THE ENNEAGRAM ROAD

An Easy and Essential Guide to Bring You Back to Complete Spiritual Wisdom, Discover the Nine Personality Types and Your True Self

Melissa Gomes

>> https://smartpa.ge/MelissaGomes<<

© **Copyright 2022 by Melissa Gomes**

All Rights Reserved.

No part of this publication may be reproduced, distributed, or transmitted in any form or by any means, including photocopying, recording, or other electronic or mechanical methods, without the prior written permission of the publisher, except in the case of brief quotations embodied in reviews and certain other noncommercial uses permitted by copyright law.
Disclaimer: This book provides accurate and authoritative information regarding the subject matter. By its sale, neither the publisher nor the author is engaged in rendering psychological or other professional services. If expert assistance or counseling is needed, the services of a competent professional should be sought.

Table of Contents

TABLE OF CONTENTS — 3

FREEBIES! — 9

   BONUS 1: FREE WORKBOOK - VALUE 12.95$ — 9
   BONUS 2: FREE BOOK - VALUE 12.95$ — 10
   BONUS 3: FREE AUDIOBOOK - VALUE 14.95$ — 10
   JOIN MY REVIEW TEAM! — 10
   FOR ALL THE FREEBIES, VISIT THE FOLLOWING LINK: — 11

I'M HERE BECAUSE OF YOU — 12

CHAPTER 1: WHAT IS THE ENNEAGRAM? — 13

   THE SYMBOLISM — 14
      The Circle: The Law of One — 15
      The Triangle: The Law of Three — 15
      The Hexad: The Law of Seven — 16
      The Nine Points — 17
   COMPLETING THE ENNEAGRAM TEST — 19
      Type Determination Exam — 20
      What to Do After Discovering Your Type — 21

CHAPTER 2:   TAKING THE ENNEAGRAM TEST — 22

   KEEPING TRACK OF YOUR CHOICES — 23
   IDENTIFYING PARAGRAPHS TO PERSONALITY TYPES — 29
      Table 1: The Paragraph Equivalents — 30

CHAPTER 3: THE ENNEAGRAM TEST FIGURE — 31

   IMPROVING RELATIONSHIPS WITH THE DIFFERENT ENNEAGRAM TYPES — 32
   HOW TO PROCEED — 32
   UNDERSTANDING THE TYPE DETERMINATION RESULTS — 33
      Parts and Definitions of the Type Connection — 34
      Type Connections — 34
      Wings — 34
      Security and Stress Types — 34
      Non-Connection Types — 35
   DEFINING THE TYPE DESCRIPTION COMPONENTS — 35
      My Type Description — 36
      Main Characteristics — 37
      My Type's Discomfort — 38
      Body-Mind-Spirit Journey — 38

Responsibility According to Personality Type	39
My Steps for Personal Development	39
Type Connection Myths	*40*
Where your Personality Type Excels	*41*
DISCOVERING YOUR TYPE AND ITS IMPORTANT FACTS	41

CHAPTER 4: PERSONALITY TYPES PART 1 - THE PERFECTIONIST AND THE HELPER   **43**

TYPE 1: THE PERFECTIONIST	43
Type Connection	*44*
Type Description	*44*
Main Characteristics of a Perfectionist	45
My Types' Discomfort	46
Body-Mind-Spirit Journey	47
Responsibility as a Perfectionist	48
Personal Development	48
Myths about the Perfectionist Type	*50*
Where Perfectionists Excel	*51*
TYPE 2: THE HELPER	52
Type Connection	*53*
Type Description	*53*
Main Characteristics of a Helper	54
My Types' Discomfort	55
Body-Mind-Spirit Journey as a Helper	56
Responsibility as a Helper	57
Personal Development	57
Myths about the Helper Type	*60*
Where the Helpers Excel	*60*

CHAPTER 5: PERSONALITY TYPES PART 2 - THE ACHIEVER AND THE LOVER   **62**

TYPE 3: THE ACHIEVER	62
Type Connections	*62*
Type Description	*63*
Main Characteristics of an Achiever	64
My Types' Discomfort	65
Body-Mind-Spirit Journey as an Achiever	66
Responsibility as an Achiever	67
Personal Development	67
Myths about the Achiever Type	*69*
Where Achievers Excel	*70*
TYPE 4: THE LOVER	71
Type Connections	*71*
Type Description	*72*
Main Characteristics of a Lover	72
My Types' Discomfort	74

Body-Mind-Spirit Journey as a Lover 75
Responsibility as a Lover 76
Personal Development 76
Myths about the Lover Type *78*
Where the Lovers Excel *79*

CHAPTER 6: PERSONALITY TYPES PART 3 - THE OBSERVER AND THE SKEPTIC 80

TYPE 5: THE OBSERVER 80
Type Connections *81*
Type Description *81*
Main Characteristics of an Observer 81
My Types' Discomfort 82
Body-Mind-Spirit Journey as an Observer 83
Responsibility as an Observer 84
Personal Development 84
Myths about the Observer Type *85*
Where Observers Excel *86*
TYPE 6: THE SKEPTIC 87
Type Connections *88*
Type Description *88*
Main Characteristics 89
My Types' Discomfort 89
Body-Mind-Spirit Journey as a Skeptic 90
Responsibility as a Skeptic 90
Personal Development 90
Myths about the Skeptic Type *92*
Where Skeptics Excel *92*

CHAPTER 7: PERSONALITY TYPES PART 4 - THE ENTHUSIAST AND THE PROTECTOR 94

TYPE 7: THE ENTHUSIAST 94
Type Connections *94*
Type Description *95*
Main Characteristics 95
My Types' Discomfort 96
Body-Mind-Spirit Journey as an Enthusiast 97
Responsibility as an Enthusiast 97
Personal Development 98
Myths about the Enthusiast Type *99*
Where Enthusiasts Excel *100*
TYPE 8: THE PROTECTOR 100
Type Connections *101*
Type Description *101*
Main Characteristics 102
My Types' Discomfort 102
Body-Mind-Spirit Journey as a Protector 103

Responsibility as a Protector	104
Personal Development	104
Myths about the ProtectorType	*106*
Where Protectors Excel	*106*
TYPE 9: THE PEACEMAKER	106
Type Connections	*107*
Type Description	*107*
Main Characteristics	107
My Types' Discomfort	109
Body-Mind-Spirit Journey as a Peacemaker	109
Responsibility as a Peacemaker	110
Personal Development	110
Myths about the Peacemaker Type	*111*
Where Peacemakers Excel	*112*

CHAPTER 8: PERSONALITY TYPE DIFFERENTIATORS — **114**

PERFECTIONISTS	116
HELPERS	117
ACHIEVERS	118
LOVERS	118
OBSERVERS	119
SKEPTICS	119
ENTHUSIASTS	120
PROTECTORS	120
PEACEMAKERS	121

CHAPTER 9: EMBODYING YOUR PERSONALITY TYPE — **123**

Maximum Self-Awareness Guide	*124*
Grounding and Centering Exercises	*125*
PRINCIPLES RELATED TO THE ENNEAGRAM	126
Three Laws of Behavior	*126*
Three Centers of Intelligence	*127*
Three Life Forces	*129*
Three Levels of Learning and Knowing	*129*
The ASAs of Growth Process	*130*

CHAPTER 10: WAYS TO REFLECT ACCORDING TO YOUR PERSONALITY TYPE — **135**

FOR PERFECTIONISTS	135
FOR HELPERS	137
FOR ACHIEVERS	139
FOR LOVERS	140
FOR OBSERVERS	142
FOR SKEPTICS	143

FOR ENTHUSIASTS 145
FOR PROTECTORS 146
FOR PEACEMAKERS 148

59 POSITIVE AFFIRMATIONS FOR DEVELOPING YOUR PERSONALITY TYPE 151

59 AFFIRMATIONS FOR DEVELOPING YOUR PERSONALITY TYPE 152

FREEBIES! 156

BONUS 1: FREE WORKBOOK - VALUE 12.95$ 156
BONUS 2: FREE BOOK - VALUE 12.95$ 157
BONUS 3: FREE AUDIOBOOK - VALUE 14.95$ 157
JOIN MY REVIEW TEAM! 157
FOR ALL THE FREEBIES, VISIT THE FOLLOWING LINK: 158

I'M HERE BECAUSE OF YOU 159

Freebies!

I have a **special treat for you**! You can access exclusive bonuses I created specifically for my readers at the following link! The link will redirect you to a webpage containing all my books and bonuses for each book. Just select the book you have purchased and check the bonuses!

>> https://smartpa.ge/MelissaGomes<<

OR scan the QR Code with your phone's camera

Bonus 1: Free Workbook - Value 12.95$

This **workbook** will guide you with **specific questions** and give you all the space you need to write down the answers. Taking time for **self-reflection** is extremely valuable, especially when looking to develop new skills and **learn** new concepts. I highly suggest you *grab this complimentary workbook for yourself*, as it will help you gain clarity on your goals. Some authors like to sell the workbook, but I think giving it away for free is the perfect way to say **"thank you" to my readers**.

Bonus 2: Free Book - Value 12.95$

Grab a **free short book** with **22+ Techniques for Meditation**. The book will introduce you to a range of meditation practices you can use to help you develop your inner awareness, inner calm, and overall sense of well-being. You will also learn how to begin a meditation practice that works for you regardless of your schedule. These meditation techniques work for everyone, regardless of age or fitness level. Check it out at the link below!

Bonus 3: Free audiobook - Value 14.95$

If you love listening to audiobooks on the go or would enjoy a narration as you read along, I have great news for you. You can download the audiobook version of *my books* for **FREE** just by signing up for a FREE 30-day trial! You can find the audio versions of my books (depending on availability) at the following link.

Join my Review Team!

Are you an avid reader looking to have more insights into spirituality? Do you want to get free books in exchange for an honest review? You can do so by joining my Review Team! You will get priority access to my books before they are released. You only need to follow me on Booksprout, and you will get notified every time a new Review Copy is available for my latest release!

For all the Freebies, visit the following link:

>> https://smartpa.ge/MelissaGomes<<

OR scan the QR Code with your phone's camera.

I'm here because of you

When you're supporting an independent author,
you're supporting a dream. Please leave
an honest review by scanning
the QR code below and clicking on the "Leave a Review" Button.

https://smartpa.ge/MelissaGomes

Chapter 1: What is the Enneagram?

The Enneagram is the foundation for understanding personality types and how people behave. While there are nine distinct personality types, most of us are a combination of two or three, so you'll also have the opportunity to learn more about yourself. This interactive workshop will help you to deal more skillfully with your colleagues and clients as you learn more about their personality types. In addition, you'll be able to identify your dominant personality traits and those of your coworkers and clients and create a strategy to navigate tricky situations at work. Through personality tests, people can better understand themselves and each other resulting in more effective communication. You can get feedback on your personality type and style and how that relates to others. You can also learn how to use the Enneagram as a tool for self and team development.

Although its origins are debatable and obscure, the Enneagram appears to have roots in various spiritual and oral traditions and a particular mathematical and intellectual heritage. Embracing your life's personal and spiritual facets can be facilitated by knowing your personality type, which can help you better understand others and yourself. As we progress in life, our personalities change and evolve, but the core characteristics and core wounds remain constant. By understanding and accepting who we are and becoming more self-aware, we can move beyond our fears and develop healthy relationships at work and with others.

Many have used the Enneagram as a practical tool in therapy and personal growth. Its insights have been used to help thousands of people heal their wounded selves and discover and embrace their true selves. It teaches people about their specific type and the "types" of everyone they know, including their parents. This knowledge helps them understand their coworkers and family members as well as themselves. For over 30 years, we have taught this comprehensive curriculum to professionals and laypeople worldwide. The Enneagram has been researched by scholars and used successfully by psychologists worldwide and is claimed to have been practiced for more than 3,000 years.

The Enneagram test explains nine recognizable and unique thinking, feeling, and behaving patterns. It is a strong and dynamic personality system that can be applied to many personal transformation and development areas.

The Symbolism

At first glance, the Enneagram is drawn as a figure with nine equidistant points resting on the circumference of a circle, depicting the continuity of life. Each of the points is connected within the circle by nine lines. Located at the top center of the circle, the top of these nine points is the tip of an equilateral triangle; the remaining six points of the diagram form an irregular hexagram symbol.

The Enneagram shows three figures: the Circle, the triangle, and the Hexad. These figures represent the three Laws of the Universe, each based on the principle of reality and its relevance to all the beings within it.

The Circle: The Law of One

The circle shape is described as a loop with no sides or stops. This figure represents the oneness of all realities that belong to the cosmos, including everything that exists or has existed in time and space and to which all living beings are a part or connected. This symbolism is called the Law of One, where the Universe includes all beings within its circle, which includes human beings and all life forms. This law expresses that all is interconnected and that the connections within the cosmos are reflected in the interconnections within an individual's psyche. Every human has a circle of people to whom they are connected; it is like a "web" of relationships or a "web of life." By becoming aware of this connection aspect within one's psyche, one can discover how certain feelings affect one's psychological state.

The Triangle: The Law of Three

The second figure is the triangle representing the principle of polarity, the interconnection of all things, and their contrasts. There are three centers of consciousness within each of us: body, mind, and spirit. These centers work together and influence each other, yet each of these centers has opposing qualities.

The body experiences pleasure and pain; the mind thinks with clarity and confusion; the spirit embraces faith and doubt. As the middle path, our spirit guides the person towards balance; it also symbolizes the Higher Being or the Highest Self, the soul, the divine principle within each human being. This part of us reaches beyond the limits of mind and body, which is represented by the upper and lower triangles of the triangle symbol. The human spirit can look within and find the path to harmony and balance in life. It possesses transcendent powers which transcend the material world and can transcend time and space. Therefore, the spirit transcends all limits; it extends beyond the body's physical boundaries. It goes beyond the mental borders of the mind and transcends the boundaries of religion and spirituality. However, this transcendence does not mean that the spirit is beyond earthly things or has no connection to material things; on the contrary, it is the connection of one's spirit with the physical and spiritual worlds.

The Hexad: The Law of Seven

The Law of Seven describes that the Universe is structured in social states of complexity. It comes with seven major aspects: seven heavens and seven layers of the Earth, seven elements and seven chakras of the human body, seven days in a week, seven days in a week of creation, seven colors of the rainbow, seven stages of spiritual development, etc. In addition, there are seven levels of consciousness in human beings that correspond to the different stages of growth. Human beings are conscious beings with different levels of awareness: subconscious, preconscious, conscious, superconscious, cosmic consciousness, Universal consciousness, and beyond human consciousness. Each level is associated with certain thoughts and feelings about reality and the world around a person.

The Nine Points

Enneagram comes from the Greek words "ennea," which means nine, and "gram," which means figure or drawing. Since ancient times, the word "ennea" has been used to refer to the nine different aspects of spiritual practices and mythologies. Our understanding of human personality continues to evolve as we study the psychological complexities of individuals from various cultures and societies; it is through the study of psychology and human behavior that the Enneagram was created. It became the study of how individuals process information and how they respond to internal and external stimuli. It also describes how people behave and feel towards others and themselves. It has been known as a tool for personality assessment and self-discovery for over a thousand years. Christian monks used it in the Middle Ages to develop self-awareness, compassion, and forgiveness toward others.

According to the Enneagram, a powerful and dynamic personality system has nine different ways of thinking, feeling, and behaving. Each of the nine patterns is founded on a fundamental idea about what we require from life to survive and be happy. These ideas are the three center points of a triangle with three sides.

Finding your Enneagram personality type will enhance your understanding of both the spiritual and personal facets of your life and help you better understand yourself and others. Whether you are interested in learning more about yourself or supporting someone in finding direction for their personal development, the Enneagram is an engaging experience.

After exploring the Enneagram in a group or on an individual basis, people report that they experience increased self-awareness; as a result, people feel more in control of their lives. The Enneagram can identify your natural and preferred ways of relating to the world, which in turn helps you gain clarity and understanding of yourself. Another advantage of the Enneagram is that it allows you to see the dynamics of your relationships and, more importantly, how it influences your behavior. It also helps you to see the results of your repetitive behaviors, which you can find in your individual or collective history. The Enneagram is a universal intelligence you cannot ignore. It will open the doors to a new and profound understanding of yourself and others that have been hidden until now.

This book contains the findings of the Essential Enneagram Test, which has been validated via significant studies. It is grounded in many scientific studies and formulated from over 40 years of research by psychologists, psychiatrists, and scholars. When using the test, we recommend that you complete the test alone and take your time to read and answer the questions truthfully and thoughtfully. Take your time to complete the entire test in one sitting. After completing the questionnaire, you will receive your type according to the Enneagram tradition. It is essential to understand you are not alone in your emotional experience and reactions; everyone is vulnerable to project energies socially. By learning to understand yourself better, you will be able to diminish the unnecessary suffering of life. It is an essential tool for personal growth and development.

A tool for developing one's self-awareness is the Enneagram personality test. Your Enneagram personality type will help you identify what you like and do not like, which drives you, and what your natural tendencies are. By understanding yourself, you can identify the social and behavioral problems you may be experiencing in your life, recognize your relationship patterns, and better know yourself as an individual. It can also help you identify what aspects of the current path you want to nurture or develop and the ones you want to let go of. The Enneagram test uses your responses to specific questions and your personality type to give you a detailed vision of how you like to live, operate in the world, and interact with others.

Completing the Enneagram test

The Enneagram Exam requires you to read nine brief paragraphs and select three different types. After reading the instructions, you will take the test. Remember to choose what type relates to you thoughtfully to understand yourself effectively. Take your time to read the paragraphs based on what you believe to be true for yourself. Each question will relate to one of the three types that you are reading. You will have to select your top three.

Enneagram test questions are designed to make you reflect on how you see yourself and the world around you. They are designed to cause reflection; therefore, your answers are based on what you truly believe and how you perceive yourself to be. After taking the Enneagram test, it is recommended to take time to review your answers along with your personality type before proceeding with the Type Determination Exam.

The Enneagram Test is an insightful personality test that helps you better understand yourself, your strengths, and your weaknesses. After taking the test, reviewing your answers to identify your personality type is a good idea. The best way to review the results is by consulting the following chapters.

Type Determination Exam

The key factors you will use to identify and validate your type are the Type Determination pages and the Type Description pages. These factors will help you identify your personality type. You will answer the questions on this page based on the Enneagram description, which you will find in the book. At the same time, your responses to the Enneagram personality test will strengthen your answers and help you identify your personality type.

Before taking the Type Determination Exam, review the Type Description pages and ensure you have selected your three most relevant personality types from the table. Once you have selected the correct type, you can read your result summary Type Identifiers. You will find the main areas or components that make up your personality type for each type. Your responses to your questions will determine if you have one or two components supporting your type's main components.

As mentioned, each of the nine types are defined in three basic points: a center point and two wings extending perpendicularly from the center point. These points are described in terms of three essential qualities that define each of the nine types. Each point has three components that contribute to the overall quality of that point. Consequently, each of the nine types consists of three basic components.

What to Do After Discovering Your Type

First, study the five guidelines all nine Enneagram types must follow, then apply the practices based on those guidelines as desired. Then read the five self-development methods linked to your unique kind, and put them into practice.

Chapter 2: Taking the Enneagram Test

The following paragraphs discuss nine personality types. I've included short descriptions of each one, along with an example. Each one of the personality types is not superior or inferior to others.

Choose three paragraphs that appear to represent you best. They are numbered from 1 to 3. Understand why you chose these paragraphs and what they represent about you. Put yourself in the first person and describe your feelings, thoughts, and behaviors. If you're having trouble deciding, consider which descriptions someone close to you would use to describe you. Now, in a paragraph of your own, write the kinds of things that happen in your brain. Focus on how they relate to your personality type. Consider similarities to how you react to situations when you face them, then refer to the paragraphs.

Remember, your paragraph needs to focus on how your personality influences how you experience life and relate to others. Imagine what someone else would see if you watched yourself for 5 minutes going through the day's routine—going to school, going to work, taking part in a social experience. Ask yourself, "Does this paragraph as a whole better match me than any of the other paragraphs?"

Keeping Track of Your Choices

After reading the paragraphs and picking the three that best describe you, write down or remember the letters of the paragraphs you chose. This step ensures you can relate to and refer back to it later.

A. I approach things in an all-or-nothing manner, especially regarding matters that are important to me. I regard to strength, honesty, and dependability highly. I don't trust others unless they've shown me to be trustworthy. I prefer straightforward communication, and I can tell when someone is being sneaky, lying, or attempting to influence me. I have difficulty tolerating people's weaknesses until I understand why they are weak or see that they are attempting to do something about it. I'm loyal and protective of my friends and tend to try to solve their problems, though sometimes it backfires and causes more problems than it solves. I'm warm, sincere, and direct in friendships and relationships. I get frustrated if people don't follow through on their promises or commitments. I can be impatient when I get things wrong. I tend to think very logically. It drives some people crazy when my explanations make sense to them but make no sense to them. People also often misunderstand my intensity. I also find it difficult to obey commands or directions if I do not respect or agree with the person in charge. I am much better at taking command of my own life. When I'm mad, it's tough for me not to show my emotions. I am always willing to defend friends, or loved ones who I believe are being treated unfairly.

B. I have high expectations for accuracy and expect myself to meet them. I may appear too judgmental or be called a perfectionist, but I try not to show it to others. I'm driven to be the best that I can be. I'm meticulous in paying more attention to details and doing things right the first time. I think logically, and I draw conclusions based on facts. I like to have things neat and organized. I make lists so I don't forget things. I'm methodical and work steadily to get things done. I don't jump to conclusions. If I were to make a list, it would probably be titled "things that I am very good at". I know I can get the job done and do what has to be done; however, I do not enjoy being busy or stressed out. It's difficult for me to ignore or accept things that aren't done correctly. I sometimes wish for more spontaneity in my actions or my relationships. I take satisfaction in the fact that if I'm in charge of anything, you can bet I'll do it correctly.

C. I tend to view things in optimistic ways and keep a good attitude toward everything I face in life. I can be flexible and take some things as they come without the stress and pressure that some of my peers face. I tend to be open-minded about most things and willing to listen to new ideas and try new activities or foods. I love to laugh and have good humor, and I like making people laugh. I'm very open-minded about different opinions, beliefs, and lifestyles. I am generally friendly and outgoing and eager to make new friends. I'm cautious about telling others how I feel because I often don't know people very well until I get to know them better. I don't like conflict and try to avoid it at all costs. I prefer to find common ground with people rather than argue about who is correct or who is right or wrong about where we stand. I need to think positively to stay calm and relaxed. I tend to be expressive and animated when talking. I enjoy a workplace where everyone works in full harmony with others.

D. I tend to be shy or reserved in new situations and keep my opinions to myself until I know what is happening and who the audience is. I like to spend time alone or in quiet places alone and do not like being the center of attention in a group setting. I tend to study before participating in new activities or when traveling to a place I've never been. I'm obedient and follow the rules. Depending upon the situation, this can either be my greatest strength or one of my biggest weaknesses. I'll follow the rules if they make sense and make sense to me, even if I do not agree with them at first. I tend to be skeptical and avoid putting my faith in something I cannot prove or believe in. I tend to be impatient when waiting for others to do something, and I can become slightly annoyed or frustrated when others do not act the way I expect. It's often easy to be aware of people's needs, especially their suffering or sadness, because I'm always there to help them as much as I'd like. It's simple for me to forgive myself. I wish I were better at saying no because I put more effort into caring for others than myself. It bothers me when people are convinced I'm attempting to influence or control them when all I'm trying to do is understand and support them. I prefer to be perceived as a warm-hearted and nice, but when I am not considered or appreciated, I can become quite passionate, even demanding. Good connections are really important to me, and I'm prepared to put in the effort to make them happen.

E. Being the greatest at what I do is a major driving force for me, and I have gotten a lot of praise for my achievements over the years. I do a lot and am effective in practically everything I try. I connect with what I do because I believe that your value is mostly determined by what you do and the praise you receive for it. I always have more to accomplish than I have time for, so I frequently put sentiments and self-reflection aside to get things done. I find sitting and doing nothing difficult since there is always something to do. I am irritated with folks who waste my time. Sometimes I'd rather just take over a project that someone is working on too slowly. I enjoy feeling and the appearance of being "on top" of any occasion. While I enjoy competing, I am also an excellent team player. I measure the amount of my self-worth by how successful I am at what I do. I am open to new ideas and like to try things. I look for opportunities to learn and improve my work skills.

F. I would define myself as a quiet, analytical person who requires more alone time than most people. I prefer to observe what is going on than to get caught up in the center of it. I don't like it when others put too many demands on me or expect me to know and report how I feel. I can connect with my feelings more when I'm alone than when I'm around others, and I often love revisiting events I've had more than while I'm going through them. I'm seldom bored when I'm alone since I lead an active mental life. It is important for me to conserve my time and energy, live a basic, straightforward life, and be as self-sufficient as possible. I highly honor my alone time. I also prefer observing people and how they react to situations than participating in them or getting involved in conflicts. I prefer to do things when I want versus letting others decide how we should spend our time.

G. I have a strong imagination, particularly regarding threats to safety and security. I can typically detect what may be harmful or destructive and either experience terror as if it were happening or just question or challenge the circumstance without experiencing panic. I either try to dodge danger or confront it head-on. In reality, because I move quickly and without hesitation, I don't often feel afraid. My imagination also contributes to my cleverness and, if not sense of humor. I'd like to have more certainty in my life, yet I seem to distrust or question the people and things around me. I am cautious of authority and am not at ease with being viewed as an authoritative figure. I like to associate with underdog causes because I can understand what is wrong with the commonly held view of things. Once I have committed myself to a person or cause, I am quite dedicated to it. I tend to have doubts or questions about things around me. I even question or doubt myself at times. I question how I fit in, what I'm here for, and what my role in life should be. I question my motives without really having a clear definition of them.

H. I am upbeat and appreciate coming up with new and exciting activities. I have a very busy mind that jumps from one concept to the next. I prefer to have a big picture of how all these ideas go together, and I get excited when I can link seemingly unrelated notions. I enjoy completing tasks that spark my interest, and I have a lot of energy to commit to them. I have a difficult time sticking with uninspiring and repeated work. I prefer to be involved in the early stages of a project when there are many great possibilities to explore. When I've lost interest in anything, it's tough to stick with it because I want to move on to the next item that has sparked my interest. If anything bothers me, I like to shift my focus to other positive thoughts. I am seldom relaxed. I am usually interested in new ideas and possibilities or plans of action that arise from these ideas. I like to be spontaneous and take full advantage of the escapades that come my way. I tend to be proactive and try to get things started in case nobody does. I can notice when people have put up façades without their awareness. I think everyone has the right to have a happy life.

I. I am a sensitive person with strong emotions. Because I am different from everyone else, I usually feel misunderstood and lonely. Others may see my actions as dramatic, and I have been criticized for being overly sensitive and overestimating my emotions. My need for emotional connection and a deeply felt relationship experience continues. I can connect with the emotional part more easily when alone than when I'm around others. Most people don't feel understood or cared for, so I strongly desire to be understood and close to someone else. My emotional reaction to things is considered unusual or childish by those around me. Because I tend to want what I can't have and hate what I do have, I have difficulties properly enjoying current relationships. The yearning for emotional connection has followed me all my life, and the lack of emotional connection has resulted in depression and frustration. I've often wondered why some people appear to have more than I do. I have a refined aesthetic sense and am involved in a universe of emotions and meaning.

Identifying Paragraphs to Personality Types

Here is a table you can refer to for your personality type according to the series of paragraphs you can relate to. Remember, you may choose multiple paragraphs that can be similar to how you behave and interact. The Enneagram has type connections that go beyond the misclassification of where your type belongs. Although the Enneagram's type system is based on psychological type theory, the research shows that most Enneagram types are not predominantly one type but a combination of several personality types.

Most Enneagram types shift somewhat from one to another, depending on their mood or circumstances. The descriptions of some of the Enneagram types overlap, so if you've identified yourself in one paragraph, it may be more accurate for you to identify yourself in another. You can refer to the list of preferences and descriptions in the next few chapters and then look at the paragraph that describes you well. If you have trouble figuring it out, try asking close people to help determine where you fit in most accurately.

Table 1: The Paragraph Equivalents

Test Paragraph	Enneagram Type	Personality
A	8	The Protector
B	1	The Perfectionist
C	9	The Mediator
D	2	The Helper
E	3	The Achiever
F	5	The Observer
G	6	The Skeptic
H	7	The Enthusiast
I	4	The Lover

Chapter 3: The Enneagram Test Figure

"Ennea" is Greek for nine, and "gram" means figure or something written. The term "Enneagram" refers to a nine-pointed star shown inside a circle. Your second and third choices indicate the stress and security associated with your personality type. The stress type is in the direction of the arrow, and the security type is away from the arrow.

The Enneagram personality system provides every child or young adult with a detailed picture of their personality, their strengths and weaknesses, and when and how their strengths are at risk. The Enneagram is also an invaluable method of learning about the personalities of parents, spouses, siblings, friends, co-workers, bosses, teachers, and coaches.

The benefits of using the Enneagram in your life are many. One major benefit is learning how to handle your emotions healthily, so the negative effects caused by emotions such as anger and stress are minimized. In the Enneagram system, there are four sets of three personality types. Another benefit is to learn how to maintain healthy relationships as a result of understanding yourself and others better.

Improving Relationships with the Different Enneagram Types

The sooner you become aware of your type, the sooner you start changing your reactions and developing more satisfying relationships. Improving relationships requires effort and common sense. To be most effective, apply the Enneagram tools to situations that bring specific emotions to mind: anxiety, stress, or anger. For example, the Enneagram will help when you are angry, anxious, tired, and confused.

The Enneagram can show you the ways you have been hurt by other people as well as the ways you hurt others. The more you receive feedback about your natural defenses and patterns, the faster you can work on your relationships. We hope this book will help you better understand yourself and your relationships and bring you closer to your healthy self.

How to Proceed

The Type Determination and Type Description details are critical to determining your personality. It is important to understand the terms of the results to assess, confirm, and validate your correct type. Take as long as you need to determine your personality type. This step is part of the process of determining your correct Enneagram type. Take your time and answer the questions as honestly as you can. After this, you will find information on how you can handle your emotions in the succeeding chapters.

Understanding the Type Determination Results

The Type Determination section helps you determine your correct personality type. As you choose your personality type in the paragraphs, resisting the temptation to give a quick answer is best to help you give a thoughtful answer.

You will often notice repeating patterns and their relationship with other personalities in the paragraphs you have read.

Enneagram Type is the number and descriptive title of each personality type. Type Determination helps you determine which types are likely to be your actual type. It also tells the alternative personalities that you may have.

For example, you might find that your personality falls between 1 and 4, so either 1 or 4 is the nearby type, and type 2 is the other. In another example, you may find that your personality type is not close to the description for any type, so 1 and 4 are the nearest types, but type 2 is more likely. Sometimes it is difficult to tell which personality type you are close to one from another. The same basic traits or behavior patterns are expressed in varying personalities. It is common to hear someone refer to themselves as not being an Enneagram type. Some people claim that they do not fit any type. This, too, is normal because the same traits or patterns can occur in any type. Think about this carefully to make sure what you think is a good fit.

Parts and Definitions of the Type Connection

The following pages tell you whether your personality is more on the type description pages just used by you or whether it favors the Type Determination details just being used by you; most likely, if the descriptions fit you best, your personality is toward these description pages.

Type Connections

Each Enneagram personality type has four connected types: the personality types associated with that personality type. These are the personalities associated with one personality type that usually agrees with three of the four descriptions from your description pages. For example, if your personality is most like Type 8, your personality agrees with three out of four of the other eight personality types descriptions. Each Enneagram personality type also has four possible types: a type from the opposite or complementary personality type categories or two personality types from the same category.

Wings

Two of the type connections are called wings, which are the personality types on either side of your type on the Enneagram figure. For instance, if you have related to being a Mediator, the types that classify as wings are Protector and Perfectionist.

Security and Stress Types

The security and stress types are the two type connections on the Enneagram. Depending on the circumstance, you shift into your security or stress type. They are defined as the following:

- The **security type** in your result is the personality that you shift to when you are relaxed or safe, and also when you feel overwhelmed.
- The **stress type** portion in your result is the go-to personality that you show when you are on the move or when you are under pressure.

Non-Connection Types

Non-connected types are personality types that look like you but are not the same. The Type Determination section will help you discover your true type. Understand that non-connected types have strong disagreements with your personality descriptions.

Defining The Type Description Components

The Type Description pages describe the nine personality types and provide information to help you understand your type. These details can give you an idea of your personality and how you can improve it. The descriptions do not mean you have to be or act exactly how the descriptions describe your type. Take the words with a grain of salt and take them in a way that fits you best. It also includes how a specific personality type commonly addresses spiritual issues and the journey ahead of them.

The Enneagram types are described in detail on two facing pages, which include the basic proposition, principal characteristics, stress, anger, and defensiveness. The Personality Type result has four key points. These key points define the character of each personality type:

1. **My Type Description**
2. **Main Characteristics**
3. **My Type's Discomfort**
4. **Body-Mind-Spirit Journey**
5. **Responsibility according to Personality Type**
6. **My Steps for Personal Development**

My Type Description

The My Type Description describes each personality type in detail and includes ideas for self-development. Under this, you have the following:

- **The basic principle I did not take into account for:** This discusses general facts that you may not have fully considered when forming your personality. You may not have considered them due to experiences in your early life.
- **Instead, I grew to believe:** The beliefs that you came in terms of from challenges and situations that happened in your life. This is where you believe things such as, "I am better than others", or "I lived all of my life feeling

completely safe." Even though you may not think you have had these beliefs, you probably did.

- **As an outcome of this belief, I adapt by:** This talks about how you interact with others and how the world sees you. This result also covers the main points needed for type description: specific traits, core energy; anger; and defensiveness.

Main Characteristics

This section of the result describes how you have built your character over the years. It also shows how you spend your time around others. These descriptions include Your basic approach: This is an attitude that someone might have about you or how someone might treat you. For example, if you are a Helper, someone might say, "She thinks everything is about her." Your basic approach is not overtly established; instead, it is believed by others based on your behavior.

Your basic approach says: This refers to what is below the surface. In other words, if you are a Controller, someone might say, "She is never satisfied." Others believe this is based on your behavior. It describes your personality in specific actions you do

- **As a result of this practice, my focus is on:** These are steps on how you coped and survived life until now. Often, this includes things you may not realize to have done consciously.
- **I put my energy into:** Habits to cope with your environment.

37

- **My good qualities:** These are the qualities that you developed over time.
- **How I talk with people:** How you express yourself to others around you.

My Type's Discomfort

This section is about how your personality reacts as it faces issues and challenges. It also describes how you look back on your past and see how you reacted. It also discusses your method for handling stress. Here, you can identify your defense mechanism when upset with other people.

- **These things bother me:** These are things that your personality stresses over.
- **These things make me mad or sad:** These are scenarios that cause anger and sorrow to you. These events are mostly from traumatic or difficult experiences in the past that you can relate to now.
- **How I express my frustration and dissatisfaction:** These include your coping mechanisms and particular desires and needs. It also describes how your type handles frustrations and how you react to fr or change.

Body-Mind-Spirit Journey

This part of the result discusses how your personality spiritually relates to the events you experience. This view can include elements of how your personality has faith, trust, and convictions regarding spirituality.

- **My spiritual journey is:** This means the practices that you do. This part also refers to what you believe spiritually. How does my type experience spirituality? These questions help you identify how you relate to spirituality and how you feel about spirituality in your personality type.
- **My path is:** How your personality type fits into the current spiritual climate.
- **My body brings me:** What your body goes through when encountering problems.

Responsibility According to Personality Type

This part of the result talks about your discipline and how it impacts your life. It describes how you react to your limitations and assets in relationships. It provides details that help you know how you judge your achievements and take responsibility for your actions. This contains what your inner critic says, which is self-explanatory: your inner judge. Inner critics judge your actions and judge your personality and your personality type. Inner critics can also voice their opinions about you as you take action. These results are the parts that help you understand yourself in things like the steps you take, how you act, and how you react. These are justifications that your mind has to make for your actions and thoughts in your life. This section of the result is a good focal point for you to find any hidden faults or biases you may have.

My Steps for Personal Development

The final section discusses how you can develop according to your personality type. If you recognize your type, this is useful information for developing or improving areas of your personality that you might struggle with before. This section includes steps you can take toward your personal goals. It includes your source of the inner self and your belief about what is important in life. Your inner source is reflected in the following points:

- **My goal to develop myself:** This is where you recall your passion for self-development and what you want to improve about yourself.
- **How I can develop myself further:** The steps, goals, and awareness that your specific personality type can do for self-development.
- **My development roadblocks:** Some core beliefs prevent you from achieving your best self. Some personalities had false beliefs about their personalities or important matters in their life. These details help you rediscover the hidden parts of your personality.
- **People can help me develop around me by:** How people can help you become better in developing yourself. This is based on your personality type and how people interact with you. This can relate to specific people, but you can also apply these ideas to everyone in your life.

Type Connection Myths

Stereotypes about each type lead to misunderstandings and rejection. Consider these false beliefs when choosing a type. This stereotype can affect the type of relationship you have with others and can damage the relationships you want.

Where your Personality Type Excels

For every personality type, there are general words that best describe them and things where they excel. You can refer to these words to see if your chosen personality type fits you. These can be positive or negative descriptions, so make sure you do not judge yourself as they may not all apply. These words are the ones that vaguely describe the type you relate to, do not limit yourself to only these descriptions.

Discovering Your Type and Its Important Facts

Keep an open mind as you take steps to discover your type. Your intuition can be a useful tool to help you know what your correct type is. Even if you have psychic abilities, you will still need to follow the detailed guide on the results to find your right type.

Your strengths and weaknesses will help you to discover your type and can include your level of satisfaction at work, with family, and friends, how money affects you, whether you're conflict avoidant or conflict-prone, your ability to be assertive, and whether you're empathetic or detached. These pages will help you discover your type, unique characteristics, and possible strengths.

Continue learning by observing your thoughts, feelings, and physical sensations and confirming and verifying your type. The Enneagram is a system for describing personality types. Using this information, you can begin the work of self-development.

Chapter 4: Personality Types Part 1 - The Perfectionist and The Helper

The beginning of your journey to personal and professional development using the knowledge of your Enneagram type. Here, you will learn how to identify and utilize your strengths, live in integrity with your type, and get clear on what you're here to do in alignment with your work, relationships, and day-to-day life experience.

Type 1: The Perfectionist

If you chose the paragraph about the Perfectionist as your first choice, you are a Perfectionist. Perfectionist people care about others and their work, although their efforts may be excessive and obsessive.

Perfectionists focus on goals, rules, and tasks and often find it hard to stop or control their impulses by focusing on the result. Perfectionists feel a little overwhelmed when they realize they're not perfect, which is the flaw or imperfection in their personality. They may also see themselves as perfectionists and others as not perfectionists. Perfectionists are vulnerable, romantic, and highly sensitive, and they can be driven to perfectionism by strong family dynamics or experiences.

Type Connection

Wings: Mediator, Helper
Security Type: Enthusiast
Stress Type: Lover
Non-Connection Types: Achiever, Skeptic, Protector

Type Description

The basic principle I did not take into account for:

We are all one and are perfect as we are.

Instead, I grew to believe:

People must hold a high standard for themselves. Good things can only happen to people who do good things. It is their responsibility to try hard to be good. I am a fixer, fault-finder, and shamer, which makes me better than everyone around me. Achievement and possession are a measure of success.

As an outcome of this belief, I adapt by:

Guarding my self-esteem by compensating and finding fault with others. If I am wrong, I correct myself with an insult or blame others and ask forgiveness. I fail to thrive unless I continually do my best to be perfect. When we are right, we feel right, and when we are wrong, we feel wrong. I am accepted in society when I am responsible and good at work. Errors must be prevented or corrected ASAP. I must meet society's expectations, no matter how high they are. I must attain my goals and do so because I must. I suppress my anger, so I tend to have resentments and develop tension.

Main Characteristics of a Perfectionist

As a result of this practice, my focus is on:

I have high standards to achieve because perfection requires it. I identify and fix flaws. I should be at my very best all the time. Guard my self-esteem by compensating and finding fault in others. Achievement and possessions are the measures of my success.

I must work hard at what I do to be successful and follow society's expectations and rules.

I put my energy in:

Control and dominance of my space and inadvertently of the people and things in my space. Taking direct action and facing conflict. Doing things the right way. Upholding important standards so that I can become self-reliant. I tend to put my personal needs and wants last to maintain integrity. I try to help others do things right, expecting them to meet the same standards I have.

My good qualities:

I am effective and responsible. As a perfectionist, I am motivated to make everything better in my life.

How I talk with people:

I question and advise based on my flawless logic. How I am in relationships: I am on guard to prevent myself and my loved ones from hurting.

My Types' Discomfort

These things bother me:

Not being able to quiet my internal critic, feeling overburdened by personal responsibility, and trying to let go of resentments. This trait makes me anxious and worried. I get upset when I do not get things right and feel like losing my power or control. I'm not too fond of the feeling of being rejected and misunderstood.

These things make me mad or sad:

- Everything I see reflects my shortcomings.
- I set high expectations for myself and others and criticized them for not meeting them.
- Comparison with the ideal is what reveals my flaws. This trait makes me very demanding.
- I feel vulnerable and exposed when I am not in control.

- Not getting anywhere with important work, being impatient, wasting resources, neglecting important tasks at work, or wanting to please everybody.
- Not being first or being the one always to win.

How I express my frustration and dissatisfaction:

As a perfectionist, I handle my frustrations by making sure that I do my jobs the right way the first time. Otherwise, I get angry and tend to curse at myself or the other person I am working with, which is not optimal. I also do not speak with the person when I am not satisfied with what they have done.

Body-Mind-Spirit Journey

My spiritual journey is:

About losing control and learning to trust.

My path is:

To listen and trust in the inner voice, even if that voice is not my own voice, and to have compassion for myself and others. I must understand that my quest for control creates so much tension in my body and spirit because it is draining and causes me so much pain.

My body brings me:

Intensity that we ignore and eventually exhaust ourselves. Undigested emotions and anger lead to enlarged glands.

Responsibility as a Perfectionist

My internal critic: Criticizes me for being imperfect and not perfect enough. Criticizes me from an external place of authority. Criticizes me for not being good or good enough to be loved. When I make a mistake, I blame myself for what I have done wrong, or I will correct myself and then blame others for my shortcomings, which highlights my insecurities and low self-esteem. My internal critics are not balanced by compassion or acceptance; consequently, I perceive myself negatively, leading to self-criticism and low self-esteem. I sometimes feel guilty about things that are not my fault. My internal critic tells me, "Be good, work harder, follow the rules, and do not make mistakes." Not allowing me any escape or relief when my self-criticism is at its peak. Sometimes this critic justifies my skills, motives, and intentions so that I can forgive myself for not being perfect enough and be kind to myself instead. My internal critic tells me I must overcome challenges with strength, willpower, and perseverance because I am not perfect. This belief leads to self-hatred and self-abuse.

Personal Development

My goal to develop myself:

48

To finally accept that chaos and imperfection are a part of the learning process. I aim to see the beauty within the chaos. To not worry so much about what others think of me or if I am good enough, I can move forward confidently. I dare to step outside my comfort zone and try new things. To realize that my willingness to take risks may also bring failures. To consider that the path toward my greatest good lies not in my certainty and clarity but in my willingness to listen, learn, and question.

How I can develop myself further:

- I can learn to accept flaws and limitations as inevitable parts of life; to accept that we will always be imperfect in one way or another; to forgive myself and others for perceived imperfections.
- I must acknowledge my strengths and accept that success cannot be fully defined or obtained; to welcome moments of failure. I have to take responsibility for my life without blaming others or circumstances.
- I have to develop the ability to discern between things that are really up to me and others to fix and those I can accept as they are.
- I must observe how I constantly monitor good and bad, accept imperfections in myself and others, let go of judgments, and allow free time for pleasure and relaxation.

My development roadblocks:

My perfectionism results in missed opportunities when I do not live up to my standards; I resent and resist anyone showing me

I'm not perfect. My compassion is one-sided and punitive toward myself, and I judge everyone else harshly by comparison. I resist self-acceptance, taking even my most special qualities for granted. I am negative toward myself or another person or group, which can be expressed with judgmental attitudes or belligerent actions. Anger and resentment block my openness to new learning and growth.

People can help me develop around me by:

Reminding me that "to err is human" and that holding a high standard for myself only limits my development. I hope that people can share their experiences about their flaws and shortcomings and how they've overcome them. Encouragement about the progress I've made and plans for future changes. Support without judgment. Help to do difficult jobs that need to be done now instead of tomorrow.

If you are not certain that the description of the Perfectionist type fits you, consider your other likely types and the myths about the type.

Myths about the Perfectionist Type

The perfectionist type is a very popular personality type. It's also not very accurate. Most perfectionists are quite lazy and unreliable. For example, the perfectionist type is often found in jobs with a lot of responsibility or people who go to college. They also tend to be very rigid and difficult to work with.

Furthermore, many perfectionists are quite bad at what they're doing. A study by personality psychologists found that up to 80% of perfectionists were unhappy with their performance. Overall, perfectionists are extremely overrated.

Where Perfectionists Excel

Perfectionists need strong self-advocacy skills to avoid perfectionistic behaviors. Perfectionism is a virtue in their upbringing, and self-discipline is highly valued. Perfectionists' heightened awareness of what is proper gives them the talent to accomplish great things. However, their perfectionism can be self-destructive or self-destructive to others. Perfectionism means too much control and a lack of spontaneity, including spontaneity in work and fun.

Perfectionists can also be overly critical, critical of others and themselves. They can judge others' work and may feel compelled to examine and correct everyone's work. Ones are often described as "neat freaks" and inflexible, but their internal standards vary greatly. These people value harmony and order, and they rob themselves of opportunities to develop their creativity or act spontaneously. Perfectionists try to please everyone and are not assertive or comfortable with conflict; they avoid confrontation and seem reluctant to ask for what they want. Perfectionists excel at planning, reason, organization, and data collection, making excellent researchers, accountants, lawyers, managers of compilations, reporters, editors, teachers, and writers - at least until they question their assumptions. Perfectionists are skilled at gathering information but less skilled at using that information to make decisions or theories or to think outside the box.

Type 2: The Helper

If the Helper paragraph was your first choice, read the Helper Type Description to see if they accurately describe your personality. If they do, you are likely a Helper.

Helpers are usually cautious, self-protective, and diplomatic; they dislike conflict and enjoy being of service to others for their gain. Helpers are often concerned about their relationships and very sensitive to what others think, and are hesitant to request what they want from others.

Usually, helpers are honest, generous, and caring. When they are criticized, they value harmony and avoid conflict.

Type Connection

Wings: Perfectionist, Achiever
Security Type: Lover
Stress Type: Protector
Non-Connection Types: Enthusiast, Mediator

Type Description

The basic principle I did not take into account for:

Accepting that everything and everyone will not be perfect. Insufficient self-care, no matter the situation, includes excessive self-sacrifice or overdoing things for others.

Instead, I grew to believe:

That you must give to receive. You have to do something in excess to receive the same amount.

As an outcome of this belief, I adapt by:

Doing more of the things that make me happy, even if this costs me time, money, energy, and sanity. The only thing that matters is whatever makes me feel good about myself, so why postpone it? You reap what you sow; somebody will certainly do something nice for me if I do something nice for them. I attach my life to the person I'm thinking about; if this person does not reciprocate, I feel sad and start to do nice things for others to try to fill the void. Because my energy and time are my biggest resources, I exert much energy or time to do things for others.

Main Characteristics of a Helper

As a result of this practice, my focus is on:

Giving my time and effort to others, proving myself, and avoiding rejection. What will make me happy has to do with others, and what gives me self-esteem depends on how many nice things I do for others. I pay attention to others and think about doing nice things for them. This trait makes me want to help people and make them happy. I routinely shift my focus from my own needs to those of others. Fearing rejection and abandonment, I aim for acceptance by pleasing others so I can win their approval and love.

I put my energy into:

Letting go of my selfish wants, needs, and desires for the pleasure of others. I am aware of my behavior instead of letting things happen. I think about others instead of myself.

My good qualities:

I love helping others with what they are going through, and others seek my help. I make it my mission to find solutions to others' problems and concerns. To make others happy, I will do almost anything. I demonstrate consistent kindness and compassion, and I become distressed when I feel others are not being treated with proper respect. I can know what it is like to be someone in pain, feeling upset, or knowing their darkest secrets, and I can help them feel better.

How I talk with people:

I am open and expressive. I listen to others well and am quick to offer my advice. Sometimes, I am seen as nosy or too helpful.

My Types' Discomfort

These things bother me:

Being rejected, abandoned, or unloved. Loss of perceived power and control. Weakness and vulnerability. The fear of becoming needy, dependent, or depressed. Feeling unloved, unattractive, unworthy, or insignificant. Not being satisfactory to others.

These things make me mad or sad: Feeling controlled, victimized, regulated, supervised, owned, restricted, or forced. I am not happy when some people do not care for others as I care for them.

How I express my frustration and dissatisfaction:

Feeling justified in being the one in control and the right; getting angry or furious; escaping, withdrawing, or letting go of a problem; relying on spirituality; overeating or eating the wrong food.

Body-Mind-Spirit Journey as a Helper

My spiritual journey is:

Being kind and helping people serve as my spiritual practice. People of faith can help me develop by encouraging me to develop my spirituality by cultivating compassion, love, and wisdom. Helping me see the connections between my serving others and my spiritual growth. Asking me to support their efforts instead of always supporting my efforts.

My path as a Helper is:

Giving myself to others, expecting nothing in return. Traveling the path of fear when I lose control. Seeking security and meaning through others.

Being compassionate. Focusing on my hardships rather than those of the people I am sacrificing. Doing things that do not make me happy, even though they might make others happy.

My body as a Helper brings me:

Pain, fatigue, resentment, exhaustion, and tension in my body. Being unable to relax or de-stress. Developing stress and feelings of inadequacy about my strength. Seeing my body as a burden or a way to earn validation and love from others.

Responsibility as a Helper

My internal critic: "You are no good; all you care about is pleasing others. You can't do anything right." I am a caring person, and I tend to forget to ask for help with my issues when I focus too much on others. I can learn that I cannot always help others and accept when others ask me to help someone. I can face the fact that my attempts to please others may always end in disappointment and accept that I may not always be able to please others or earn their love. I can accept that I am important to myself and that I will always make mistakes. As a helper, I allow myself to be controlled or dominated by people. I suffer alone in private. I can learn how to value myself through my experiences. I can learn how to nurture myself and take care of myself first. I can learn how to protect myself from the hurtfulness of others and from my habits of pleasing others to avoid their disappointment.

Personal Development

My goal is to develop myself:

To accept and understand other people's points of view; to relinquish my ideas, feelings, and judgments. I wish to express gratitude and appreciation without appearing desperate for their care or attention. Developing the ability to be non-judgmental of others' human weaknesses. Knowing that others make mistakes and that we all are on our paths. Being a self-advocate for myself and not putting my needs behind me. I express gratitude to others for their support and show that I am willing to seek help when needed. Learning to choose what I need and want instead of being controlled by external circumstances. Accept that I have needed it even if I do not always show them. Giving others space to be themselves instead of always trying to please them. Find outlets for my anger, frustration, and resentment so they will not affect the quality of service I provide to my family and friends.

How I can develop myself further:

- To take care of my own needs, not on other people's terms but according to the value of my individual needs for rest, relaxation, and pleasure.
- To treat me with compassion and kindness and to speak up in self-advocacy. To ask for help when I need it, not when others think I should need it.

- Close the gap between my selflessness and my selfishness.
- Let go of my need for others' approval and validation and feel safe in who I am.
- To see what others can see in me: my essence, my worth, my value, my gifts, and my compassion.
- To take care of other's needs as an expression of love or responsibility without putting aside my own needs or desires.
- To shift my primary focus from pleasing others and caring for them so much to the pursuit of my own joy.
- Accept that I don't have to take care of everything and have the right to care for myself.
- Expecting some rejection of my invitations or offers to do things and adapting my responses accordingly.
- Accept that I am imperfect and others may not appreciate my efforts.
- Practicing connecting with my feelings instead of repressing them.

My development roadblocks as a Helper:

Feeling bad about taking time for my own needs or for not being as giving as I wish to be. Fear of being rejected if I ask for help. Fear of putting people on notice that I take them for granted.

People can help me develop around me by:

Asking me if I need help with anything. Providing support when I seem to ask for it indirectly. Affirming and valuing my commitments and accomplishments. Reminding me to take time for myself and not ignore my needs and feelings. Others must understand that I sometimes need to say no to others because I am giving my all at the time.

If you are unsure about your type, consider the other probable types and the myths about types.

Myths about the Helper Type

Helpers are often described as selfless, excessively serving others, and sacrificing themselves for the well-being of others. However, they seem to do it mainly to manipulate people into liking them. Helpers are more concerned with appeasing others than doing what's right; they may manipulate others by using guilt to get their way. They think more about what is best for others than what's in their best interest and become unable to distinguish their needs from those of others.

Helpers usually become exhausted from giving so much to others and resentful toward people they've given too much to. Many helpers eventually develop passive-aggressive tendencies in expressing their anger without saying they're angry. They are often considered "people pleasers."

Where the Helpers Excel

Helpers often sit back and let others make decisions because they're afraid of confrontation, have low self-esteem, or fear losing control. They are drawn to helping professions because it seems they would help people, but they often passively serve people for their gain. As helpers tend to help people out whenever they can, they may seem helpful and kind but weak-willed and passive-aggressive, and they may lose their sense of self-respect. They are usually quite skilled in diplomacy and can disarm difficult people without making them mad; they may even use "seduction in reverse" to get what they want. Giving is often the best way to earn people's trust and loyalty. People are often drawn to a helper's good nature and trust them. People like helpers have an automatic tendency to please others. People also expect the characteristic qualities that give the helpers devotion, reliability, and trustworthiness.

Chapter 5: Personality Types Part 2 - The Achiever and The Lover

In this chapter, we will discuss the Achiever and the Lover personality types.

Type 3: The Achiever

If the Achiever paragraph was your first choice, read the following pages to learn more about your personality. The Achiever measures their success by how much they are achieving in life. They are driven, goal-oriented and ambitious.

Achievers are very productive with their life goals. Most people like this personality type because they are very decisive and can complete tasks efficiently and on time. They work well in groups because they typically contribute well and know how to motivate others.

Type Connections

Wings: Helper, Lover
Security type: Skeptic
Stress type: Peacemaker
Non-Connection Types: Enthusiast, Perfectionist, Protector

Type Description

The basic principle I did not take into account for:
The laws of the Universe make everything work naturally. Nothing should be forced.

Instead, I grew to believe:
It depends on the person on what will be done. Our achievements depend on what we do in life.

As an outcome of this belief, I created the below adaptive strategy:
I can achieve anything I want in life as long as I work hard enough. Because of this belief, I see life as a giant obstacle course racing through our life to achieve our goals. I am successful when obstacles can be conquered, and goals are achieved. I am successful when hard work pays off.

This belief results from the need to do as much as possible before resting. My goals are my primary focus, and I work hard to achieve them. It means that I always have something to do with my life. If I do not have a goal with immediate thought, I will create one to replace it with.

Main Characteristics of an Achiever

As a result of this practice, my focus is on:
I have high standards to achieve because perfection requires it. I identify and fix flaws. I should be at my very best all the time. Guard my self-esteem by compensating and finding fault in others. Achievement and possessions are the measures of my success. I must work hard at what I do to be successful and follow society's expectations and rules.

I put my energy in:
Being busy more than relaxing because I enjoy the feeling of accomplishment that comes with the work I achieve. I enjoy being productive and the achievement that comes with working hard. I organize my activities to be efficient and productive. I enjoy the adrenaline that comes with meeting deadlines and solving complex problems. It is to show others that even though I may be focused on worldly things.

My good qualities:
I can finish tasks ahead of time. I perform well under pressure. I can be both efficient and productive. I work well on a team and enjoy being aware of and controlling my work and environment. I work hard, and many of my goals are achieved. achieving goals is extremely important to me. I am generally productive and always busy with work and need to stay busy. I am an achiever. I enjoy the feeling of productivity that comes with meeting deadlines and completing tasks at work. I can both tackle big goals and implement daily jobs efficiently.

How I talk with people:
As an achiever, I talk with people directly and in a fast-paced manner. People see me as smart and capable when I confidently talk to them. I focus on the matter, speak about issues, and leave emotions off the list. I thrive on change because it keeps me focused, and I rarely fear it.

My Types' Discomfort

These things bother me:
When conflicts arise, I am swift with my decision and actions. I can resolve most disagreements on my own. Because I make my goal my top priority, I am often seen as being overbearing and dominating.

These things make me mad or sad:
I get upset when things do not go my way or if it takes me longer to achieve my goal than it did for other people. I am unpleasantly surprised when things do not happen when I think they should happen because they usually do not. I hate being wrongly criticized. I can be passive-aggressive in retaliation or ignore what I do not like. Because of my drive to achieve, many things slide on my to-do list.

Things that make me happy:
Getting my situational goal finally accomplished. Not achieving my goals makes me feel inadequate. I become very frustrated and angry if I have not completed something on my list for the day. I get mad when I feel I am not getting what I want. Being told that my expectations are too high is insulting because it

implies that I am either lazy or do not care about my potential. Being told I am not trying hard enough is an insult. Getting negative feedback makes me want to work harder.

How I express my frustration and dissatisfaction:
I become impatient and irritable when I do not accomplish tasks as quickly as I would like. I become very frustrated when fewer opportunities come my way than other people. When I am confronted, I tend to retreat and reevaluate my objectives.

Body-Mind-Spirit Journey as an Achiever

My spiritual journey is:
About learning how to engage or revert on tasks or situations.

My path is:
To become helpful to everyone and to achieve things that are meaningful and fulfill me. My spiritual objective is to master my mind and body through practice, training, and education to be able to help or help others in achieving their goals in life. I hope to transform my mind and body into a form that I can wish to master.

My body brings me:
I am physically affected by turbulence and stress. If I am stressed, my body and mind become sick with tension, ulcers, anxiety, insomnia, headaches, and lung problems.

Responsibility as an Achiever

My internal critic:
It accuses me of not doing enough. I am not feeling good enough and being lazy. I look for freedom and independence in implementing my work whenever possible. I always want to complete my goal as fast as humanly possible. I face my shadow self as working hard but being perfectionistic and constantly encountering obstacles. My responsibility is to control myself and be aware of my thoughts, feelings, and emotions.

Personal Development

My goal to develop myself:
To finally accept that chaos and imperfection are a part of the learning process. I aim to see the beauty within the chaos. I can move forward confidently by not worrying about what others think of me or if I am good enough. I dare to step outside my comfort zone and try new things. To realize that my grit in taking risks may also bring failures. Know that the path toward my best version lies not in my certainty and clarity but in my eagerness to listen, learn, and question.

How I can develop myself further:
- I can learn to accept flaws and limitations as inevitable parts of life; to accept that I am always imperfect in one way or another; to forgive myself and others for perceived imperfections.
- I must acknowledge my strengths and accept that success cannot be fully defined or obtained; to welcome

moments of failure. I have to take responsibility for my life without blaming others or circumstances.

- I have to develop the ability to discern between things that are really up to me and others to fix and those I can accept as they are.
- I must observe how I constantly monitor good and bad, accept imperfections in myself and others, let go of judgments, and allow free time for pleasure and relaxation.

My development roadblocks:
I get sidetracked when I do not achieve my goal and stay focused on the negatives. I feel alienated when I do not easily grasp or understand the process.

People can help me develop around me by:
Encourage me to pay attention to feelings and relationships by being supportive and letting me know what is important to others. Show me that someone cares about me for who I am, not just what I achieved. Remind me to slow down sometimes and relax.

If you are not sure of matching the details of the Achiever type, consider your other likely types and the myths about the type. Becoming more conscious about your own behavior gives you insight into how others perceive you.

Myths about the Achiever Type

The Achiever is a type who fears being liked, lacking skills, or being viewed as lazy and stupid. The Achiever types work extra hard to ensure that people will accept them. They might seem shy or withdrawn and like secret things to be kept inside.

Unlike the commonly known, the Achiever type works well in teams, is willing to go out on a limb, and tries to manage her emotions. These types can easily compartmentalize their lives into social lives, work lives, lives with partners, and other aspects. As they can always keep a balance even when something goes wrong in life, Achievers also do not lose my dedication or motivation. In addition, people who have this type of personality also have an ability to be critical of themselves and not show it to others.

Achievers are special, amazing people who do not need to worry about what people think about them because they are always confident. They do whatever they have to do to achieve goals, even if it involves self-sacrifice or self-denial, even to the point of studying for an exam instead of watching TV.

Where Achievers Excel

Achievers excel in military, law enforcement, fire-fighting, law enforcement, and emergency services. They take charge and make decisions when they see the need for leadership and command. They rely on experience to guide them instead of textbooks, and sponsors are usually quick to recognize and appreciate an Achiever's determination and perseverance.

People with the Achiever personality type can succeed in business as long as they focus on identified goals and remain after others give up or stop trying. Achievers often work as consultants because of their drive, ability to listen, and ability to solve complex problems. They can positively affect people around them because they motivate these types to do their best. Careers that require high competitiveness are where the Achievers excel in. They appreciate things when they reach a standard or level of performance. These people can achieve even more when they mentally challenge themselves to perform at a ridiculously high level. Achievers contribute greatly to the world of sports because they expect and demand more from themselves. They need to see exactly what has to be done to accomplish results. These types enjoy competition when they can see win and fail. They are hard to coach because they are highly self-motivated and must be persuaded to progress before they want to turn a corner.

Type 4: The Lover

If the Lover paragraph was your first choice, there is a high possibility that this is your type. Read the following Lover details to learn more about this type.

Lovers, as an Enneagram type, are unusually good at communicating feelings and emotions and thus good at being therapists, counselors, coaches, ministers, and teachers. People often seek their advice because they are good listeners. They are also good at communicating ideas or thoughts through deep reflection and personal understanding.

Lovers prioritize developing communication skills. They are natural storytellers who respond best when others emotionally challenge them to talk about their emotions. By sharing their gained deep personal knowledge and understanding, they can encourage others and teach them to understand themselves and others better.

Type Connections

Wings: Achiever, Observer
Security type: Perfectionist
Stress type: Helper
Non-Connection Types: Enthusiast, Skeptic, Peacemaker

Type Description

The basic principle I did not take into account for:
Everything and everyone in this world is connected on a deeper level.

Instead, I grew to believe:
Some people feel abandoned when they experience unbearable loss to their original connections.

As an outcome of this belief, I adapt by:
The ideal love will sustain me. As long as I have that person in my life, I will be okay. My willingness to take risks may also bring failures. To consider that the path toward my greatest good lies not in my certainty and clarity but in my willingness to listen, learn, and question.

Main Characteristics of a Lover

As a result of this practice, my focus is on:
I long for what I do not have at this point in my life. I also tend to review the past and imagine the future. I care about what happened before and what is about to happen, not the present. I evaluate future situations to my liking; I might base it on an experience or a distant fantasy. I focus on pleasing others, avoiding conflict, and not being seen by other people as anxious.

Consequently, I suppress my anxieties and feelings, which sometimes erupt later in a tirade or a major perceived injustice.

I put my energy in:

I always look for fulfilling connections and a deeper meaning in life. I try to connect things by thinking about how they feel about each other or how they affect each other. My capacity to relate with others is limited by the efforts of my expectations and demands. I know I can change how I feel by changing how I think. I learn from experiences, relationships, and memories. I do think about the future. But I have trouble doing it because it is mostly based on theories and fantasies.

My good qualities:

I value being loved. I look for someone with whom I can build a bond. For me, being loved and respected means being a certain kind of person. I manage to overcome my fears, doubts, and anxiety. I can grow more as I let go of expectations, worry, pressure, and striving. From this freed space, and because I have openness toward feelings, I can connect deeply with others.

How I talk with people:

As a Romantic type, I focus on my feelings and emotions. I will express strong feelings when discussing what happened. I do not judge others. Always wanting someone to understand me and to influence others' behaviors and perceptions is a vital need in my existence. I will struggle with what I perceive as indifference. I may seem vulnerable, but am not my usual candid self.

How I connect with others:

I am sensitive to the comfort of others. Growing up, I often had to become tough and strong early to compensate for my fears. Many things scared me when I was younger. A lack of self-confidence has been part of being a young Romantic. After many years of struggling to overcome my insecurities and fears, I have become more courageous. But I do not forget that being open and showing my feelings is a weakness. I work hard to ensure I am behaving in a certain way that others might recognize as masculine and, at the same time, try to keep my emotions under control. Being a Helper makes me accessible to others, especially those who need emotional support but do so in my weak states.

My Types' Discomfort

These things bother me:
I am bothered when I see someone that does not care about others. I am bothered by people who offer to help but do nothing to help. I am bothered by feeling inferior compared to those around me. I am bothered by having to face difficult situations. I am bothered by feeling invisible when I feel I should matter. I am bothered by being judged as better or worse than my brother, son, father, mother, teacher, and friend. I am bothered by being that one person that everyone wants, but no one wants to be with.

These things make me mad or sad:
Sometimes, I feel sorry for myself, my suffering in life, or people's judgment toward me because of it. Maybe I spend too much time focusing on others and what they think of me or

what they do to me. I sometimes turn my mind away from thinking things through and let myself go with the flow.

How I express my frustration and dissatisfaction:
I sometimes find myself saying or writing things I regret later. I can be critical, which makes me feel better momentarily, but leaves others upset. I hide my feelings by withdrawing attention and becoming cold.

I try to please others and avoid conflict. I do not ask for help unless I know I cannot do the job well. I ask others for help when needed, but I rarely take the initiative. I avoid doing or making imperfect things. I could help but not to the extent that I could cause someone else harms. I stay in the background and wait for someone to come to talk to me - even if they don't.

Body-Mind-Spirit Journey as a Lover

My spiritual journey is:
As a Lover, I dedicate myself to growing spiritually by searching for meaning in my life. I honor my connection to the Universe and ask it to guide me in my life. I become more open and more loving toward others. I am faithful to my commitments in life and love. I grow emotionally and share more deeply those things that enrich me spiritually and bring me happiness.

My path as a Lover is:
I recognize that I am using the past to frame my feelings in the present and the future. I acknowledge my deep need to connect

and nourish myself by practicing compassionate meditation. My future self reminds me that I am still the same person I was before, but I have experienced a transition.

My body as a Lover brings me:
Chest pain, tension headaches, and cervical strain during times that I think too much. Muscle tension and pain related to holding my stress in my legs. My chest area hurts if I hold emotions in for too long. My head hurts, neck and shoulders ache. I feel tense in the upper part of my body and heart area. Tension headaches and neck pains when I overemphasize the importance of my ideas.

Responsibility as a Lover

My internal critic:
I am not good enough. I do not have enough self-discipline, and I am a slob. I am hopeless, and don"t deserve better. I am too needy or too demanding. I hold myself back from having what I want. I am too sensitive. I am too timid to say what is right. I am too single-minded. I am too focused on my past or future self that I forget the now. I am too serious about life. I am too much work.

Personal Development

76

My goal to develop myself:

As a Lover type, I can search for meaning in anything that touches me. I develop my spirituality by listening to my heart – and by listening to other people as well. My heart expands when I focus on how I can make someone's life better. When I feel fulfilled spiritually or emotionally, I feel like the whole world is open to me.

How I can develop myself further:

- By transforming my thoughts and emotions, I can let go of the things that block my ability to love and be loved.
- Starting to see my inner being and my potential as lovable and loving will help me to let go of my need to be special or better than others. This means acknowledging my talents and developing them - while simultaneously accepting them as they are.
- I want to develop myself by working to create unforgettable moments for others and myself. I can become someone of value by adopting a more giving attitude. I can laugh more, live more pleasantly, and forgive more easily.
- By discovering new perspectives, I can transform my emotions. I can love someone with compassion and self-love.
- I am touched by the compassion and openness of people who genuinely care about and understand me. My ability to confront and overcome my struggles helps me feel like life is worth living.

My development roadblocks:

I worry about how others perceive me. I have a fear of rejection. I don't always see eye to eye with others when learning how to share the love. When I'm not in love, I sometimes feel alone, that my life has no meaning or purpose. I become defensive whenever I hear any criticism about who I am and what I do; I criticize myself as well. Sometimes I am afraid to risk losing what I have. Sometimes I just want to hide or escape from life for a while.

People can help me develop around me by:
Encourage me to focus on the now. Honor my emotions and input. Support my efforts in seeking meaning in life. Help me express my creativity, emotions, and ideas in life's celebrations. Let me find ways to connect more deeply with others. Support me in relaxing, laughing and being playful, and having fun. Help me stretch myself beyond my comfort zone.

Becoming aware of your type helps you understand what drives your behavior and allows you to improve your life.

Myths about the Lover Type

Lovers are believed not to think and just trust their emotions fully. While inclined to their emotions more, these personality types do more things with dedication. Not everyone likes a Lover personality because they are more cautious and detail-oriented than other types. They have good intuition and are always concerned about how others feel.

Where the Lovers Excel

People with the Lover personality type communicate warmth and compassion through words and actions. They listen to others and share their discoveries about themselves and the world around them. Lovers enjoy helping others feel emotionally safe and showing love to their loved ones through compassion and empathy. Nurturing and supporting others to grow and develop mentally and physically is a Lover type's goal, along with filling their lives with interesting and meaningful activities, hobbies, and relationships. They tend to be curious about life, people, nature, and the world around them.

Chapter 6: Personality Types Part 3 - The Observer and The Skeptic

This chapter talks about the Observer and Skeptic personality types and how they are similar and different from each other.

Type 5: The Observer

If the Observer paragraph was your first choice, read the following pages to learn more about your personality. The Observer measures their accomplishments by whether the project is completed successfully. If an Observer is in charge of a large team, they remember every mistake and are quick to point it out to the entire team. If there is a problem that they cannot immediately solve, they demand that the problem is reported to them for resolution.

This personality type usually leaves detailed written instructions to be followed closely by those working with the Observer. An Observer has a knack for knowing when a project is ahead of schedule and knows when it is running behind. This personality type is more cautious and needs high-pressure situations to help them to perform at their best. The Observer personality type is not aggressive or controlling. They are naturally good at delegating and work well as a team. These personalities are honest and do what they say they will do.

Type Connections

Wings: Skeptic, Lover
Security type: Protector
Stress type: Enthusiast
Non-Connection Types: Perfectionist, Peacemaker

Type Description

The basic principle I did not take into account for:

Everything I need from the Universe can be provided by the right means.

Instead, I grew to believe:

People in our existence want everything for themselves, leaving others empty and forgotten.

As an outcome of this belief, I adapt by:
I keep my privacy to save myself from being abused. I'm distrustful of my environment. I take care of myself, so I can care for others. I act in my best interest to protect myself from others.
Main Characteristics of an Observer

As a result of this practice, my focus is on:
Valuing stability and continuity. I don't mind breaking routines, but I need continuity. I welcome change. New ideas excite me. When exploring different possibilities, I always follow what I have observed as right.

I put my energy in:
Working with people and having a natural ability to relate to people. I view people as individual and unique. I find connections with people and situations easily.

My good qualities:
I value relationships but maintain control of my environment. I love to ponder new ideas and situations, but when it comes to action, I can take charge like a boss when it comes to action. I understand that change is inevitable, so I am ready to adapt quickly to new experiences.

How I talk with people:
As an Observer, I observe people's actions, thinking, and feelings to explore their interactions. As the conversation progresses, I respond to the connections and opportunities for action I see in the other person's responses.

My Types' Discomfort

These things bother me:

I function well under pressure, but I do not like things to be dire. I become more serious and focused to the point that I turn people away.

These things make me mad or sad:

I get mad when there are too many emotions around me. If I don't have enough time for myself, I cannot focus, which makes me sad or mad.

How I express my frustration and dissatisfaction:

I withdraw from the situation and the other person to avoid conflict and stress. However, I become assertive when the situation becomes too uncomfortable. I don't take action by force when possible. Once I resolve or distance myself from the issue, I regain my focus and can move on with my life. When I work under pressure, I will complete the issue quickly and move on.

Body-Mind-Spirit Journey as an Observer

My spiritual journey is to:
Observe the restrictions and boundaries of my mind. I also need to observe and come to terms with my fear of the unknown and my need to control everything. I need to overcome my shallow beliefs on how I should live my life and release the self-imposed expectations of others, and trust that I could succeed.

My path as an Observer is to:
Develop unconditional love for myself and expand it to include other people.

My body as an Observer brings me:
Depression and anxiety. My metabolism also gets affected because I am usually in seclusion and prefer sitting down when I need to focus.

Responsibility as an Observer

My internal critic: I need to present myself to people properly. I try to avoid a reserved personality, but people will respect me more when they know I am direct and honest. During stressful situations, I might have less patience and keep trying to control the situation and the outcome more when under pressure.

Personal Development

My goal to develop myself:

I must develop self-confidence in my beliefs and my ability to achieve my goals while still putting others' needs above mine. By developing my self-confidence, I make myself a role model for others, giving them the confidence to believe they can take risks in conquering their fears.

How I can develop myself further:
- I need to open up to people and accept their help when they offer it.
- I also need to bring more enthusiasm into situations and my interactions with others.
- I will be better at listening to others and at understanding when there is a need for me to take action.
- I need to include myself in more social situations.
- I willsupport and take more opportunities to reach my goals.

My development roadblocks:
I sometimes don't ask for help or discuss personal issues when I badly need support from others. I also get distracted when there is a lot of confusion and disarray.

People can help me develop by:
We can help each other if we understand that each person has a path to walk. I appreciate people who value me but are not afraid to tell me when I do something wrong. Have a more open attitude towards me so I can explore my opportunities.

Myths about the Observer Type

People with the Observer personality type are passive dipsticks who don't care about other people. The Observer personality type, however, is always there for everyone, but they need comfortable and consistent environments in which they can perform.

Where Observers Excel

Observers excel in situations where people have a sense of discipline or when their leadership skills are needed. They are very nurturing and sensitive toward others. They can come up with the exact amount of input needed to ensure that the assignment meets with everyone's approval. They love taking charge and making decisions, and their work is usually completed efficiently, ensuring everyone has a good time in the process.

The Observer types love to analyze situations thoroughly. Like a river, when the Observer takes a path, it is less traveled and is not the typical path the type takes. This personality type likes to see where the path leads and will consider possibilities others would not even consider. Their natural curiosity allows them to learn anything new and experience new options. The Observer types are creative problem solvers and are good leaders. This personality type naturally thinks before taking action and can see long-term outcomes and options others do not see.

The Observer's stay-the-course philosophy is like the thrill of rock climbing and jumping from a high place. The challenge and risk of falling keep the Observer on their toes. This personality type likes the feeling of not knowing what will happen next and having to make choices as they go along. This personality type knows how to turn challenges into positives. For those who are used to the Observer's cautious, focused attitude, it can be interesting and refreshing to be with someone who always pushes themselves outside the box.

Type 6: The Skeptic

If the Skeptic paragraph was your main choice, read further and learn more about your personality type. The Skeptic type measures success by whether a project is finished by following their standards. If a Skeptic is in charge, they are very careful to hire a professional for a task that they know little about but often still question their capabilities.

Skeptic types are usually confrontational and blame others when things go wrong. When they cannot solve problems, they immediately turn their sights on the person who caused the problem. People with this personality type have a talent for quickly identifying the details of a project and will always, with few exceptions, get the project completed after repeated criticism until it is perfect in their eyes.

Type Connections

Wings: Observer, Skeptic
Security type: Peacemakers
Stress type: Achiever
Non-Connection Types: Lover, Protector

Type Description

The basic principle I did not take into account for
We must believe in ourselves and the natural process of the Universe, wherever it may lead.

Instead, I grew to believe:
Too many uncertain things happened in my life, and it isn't easy to trust the Universe.

As an outcome of this belief, I adapt by:
I question everything around me. I try to be part of the solution when problems arise, but I must feel protected and in control.

Main Characteristics

As a result of this practice, my focus is on:
Identifying and correcting any mistakes I might make.

I put my energy in:
Watching others' movements and my own. I always need to make sure that everything is done how I picture it happening.

My good qualities:
I quickly find faults, and I correct them quickly to eliminate errors. I am good at thinking on my feet and through complex issues.

How I talk with people:
I handle situations in a way that makes sense to me. I explain things and expect that others will follow suit. I don't express dissatisfaction, I express dissatisfaction calmly and constructively. I don't become defensive until I sense that my approach or skill is somehow being challenged.

My Types' Discomfort

These things bother me:
Sometimes, I worry too much or can't let go of a problem.

These things make me mad or sad:
I don't like to be corrected or to have my ideas challenged.

How I express my frustration and dissatisfaction:
I become quiet and try to change the subject. I even become so upset that I forget to think clearly, which brings more problems. My issues often leave me sad when I do not get the outcome I am looking for. I become aloof and silent and do not quickly find solutions or why I should trust the situation.

Body-Mind-Spirit Journey as a Skeptic

My spiritual journey is:
Finding something to believe in. Whether it is a common belief or my own, I must establish this in myself to become consistent.

My path as a Skeptic is:
To try to solve every problem until the problem is solved despite everything in the process that I question.

My body as a Skeptic brings me:
Headaches, and I get upset and sad. I tire easily and have a short attention span. I am impatient when things do not happen as I picture them and my judgment may be wrong sometimes.

Responsibility as a Skeptic

My internal critic: "There is a better way to do things." I judge myself against other people. My health has been poor most of my life. I have a hard time dealing with people who make important decisions for me.

Personal Development

My goal to develop myself:
To realize that not everything is in my power to control. I aim to take responsibility for myself as well as for others. I will overcome my obstacles by developing faith, trusting in the Universe, and that other people's intention is good.

How I can develop myself further:
- I should not fear change.
- I can develop by letting go of my need to control everything.
- I need to break through my fear of the unknown so that I can develop curiosity and the courage to tackle new issues and situations.
- I must accept others' methods in working with me instead of always making suggestions so that I can most effectively be the reliable person I need.

My development roadblocks:
As a skeptic, I'm not sure if I can trust people to help me develop. This belief is also why I am also skeptical in the first place.

People can help me develop by:
Always providing proof of their beliefs to me, and keeping me informed of others' conclusions. In turn, people must also trust my ideas because if I question something, it must be a real concern. People need to understand that my need to control can positively impact me and others.

Myths about the Skeptic Type

The Skeptic personality type is angry control freaks who are never satisfied. The Skeptic personality type, however, is the person in charge, and they like making sure that everyone does what they are asked to. They are trustworthy, reliable, loyal, and courageous. They are clever at working with fact-oriented people who are very critical of their ideas and work. They dislike having to explain their reasoning, and they often prefer logic to death-defying impulses. They have an innate ability to foresee potential issues and to plan ahead, enabling them to do their job well.

Another myth about Skeptics is that they criticize everything, but this is incorrect. Skeptics are extremely critical, but they do not criticize what they cannot prove and believe that everything has a purpose. They will criticize general procedures that they consider irrational, improper, or otherwise unacceptable, but they will not personally attack someone simply because they do not use logical reasoning.

Remember, a Skeptic will not tolerate operations that are slow, sloppy, or done without integrity because these are the hallmarks of the Skeptic's personality type.

Where Skeptics Excel

Skeptics excel in demanding environments, such as high-stress laboratories or large corporations, where perfection is expected, and everything is standardized. Skeptics should be aware of their tendency toward controlling others and should try to develop a more sympathetic nature if that is not their strength. To accomplish this, they should take themselves out of their work environment as much as possible and spend time developing their patience with others through organizing, helping, or participating in community volunteer work.

Skeptics also excel in careers where they use their excellent time management and organizational skills or where they can use their intense listening skills to help their clients succeed. These careers include engineering and educational services and anything that requires a methodical approach because it involves making decisions based on logical issues such as education, politics, or social issues.

Skeptics are particularly good at the height of analysis when their ability to pinpoint solutions to complex problems and use their extraordinary powers of logic and deduction comes into play. They are meticulous, flexible, independent, and decisive in their approach to problem-solving and like to fix issues through a process of elimination and logic. They enjoy math and science as well as careers where they must meet high standards of quality or productivity, such as research and development. Excellent careers for Skeptics include computer programmers, professional counselors, public relations specialists, school administrators, biologists, urban planners, architects, chemists, researchers, document examiners, and nuclear engineers.

Chapter 7: Personality Types Part 4 - The Enthusiast and The Protector

This chapter explains the final three personalities in the Enneagram personality test. As a personality often develops according to the way it perceives the world, how others perceive it also affects a person's personality.

Type 7: The Enthusiast

The Enthusiast type is generally cheerful and has a positive outlook in life. They have high energy and are always enthusiastic when talking about their interest areas. However, their high interests can wear out others, and the Enthusiast may find themselves being taken advantage of by others. They are easily confused and have difficulty filtering out the unimportant things in their lives.

Type Connections
Wings: Skeptic, Protector
Security type: Observer
Stress type: Perfectionist
Non-Connection Types: Helper, Peacemaker, Achiever

Type Description

The basic principle I did not take into account for:

Things in life are possibilities to be experienced.

Instead, I grew to believe:

Limits are set for people. This causes them distress and often upsets them.

As an outcome of this belief, I adapt by:

I engage in activities that I enjoy and want to experience everything at once. The problem with adapting to this new belief is that people have different interests and therefore do not always want to participate in the same activities as me. Sometimes, I soon discover that I no longer like the person's interests and activities, so I simultaneously engage in many different activities. People frequently leave me behind because I want to avoid forming a true commitment to one thing.

Main Characteristics

As a result of this practice, my focus is on:

I want to enjoy all the good things in life and experience them all at once.

I put my energy in:
I like learning many things at once. It's a good practice for me to be "a jack of all trades." I enjoy everything that life offers me. As a result, I tend to be an eager learner.

My good qualities:
I get easily excited and enthusiastic about new subjects and interests. I enjoy active learning and have high energy and creativity. Enjoy good company and great experiences. Enable others to switch easily between subjects and activities. I quickly learn from my mistakes and can pick up new tasks faster. I can prioritize effectively and quickly complete things that I focus on.

How I talk with people:
I tend to talk to people in a light-hearted way, so they do not always pay attention to what I have to say. Therefore, it's usually necessary for me to use humor or remind them about some funny stories when communicating with them.

My Types' Discomfort

These things bother me:
I get upset with people that do not share my enthusiasm in life. I become impatient with people who do not have the same interests as me. It's also difficult to cope with all the things that I take part of sometimes.

These things make me mad or sad:
I hate having limits. People who do not appreciate things I am interested in make me upset or angry.

How I express my frustration and dissatisfaction:
I try to ignore my fear or anxiety because I do not take it seriously. Instead, I focus on something positive and positive about a situation or person. I also avoid negative people or situations when I get angry or upset by engaging in activities I enjoy.

Body-Mind-Spirit Journey as an Enthusiast

My spiritual journey is:
I must focus on all aspects of an experience and follow my interests actively.

My path is:
I want to learn many things anywhere in the world and enjoy activities.

My body brings me:
I feel exhausted at the end of the day. Fatigue is common to me.

Responsibility as an Enthusiast

My internal critic:
I am easily discouraged by negative people, so I come back home to get my head straight. I become restless when I have to deal with negative situations.

Personal Development

My goal is to develop myself:
I develop the skills to embrace many activities and people. I want to find a balance between social activities and work activities.

How I can develop myself further:
- I must practice working on one thing at a time until it is completed, living life more fully in the present moment and less in the future, and practicing loving-kindness.
- I want to reconnect with people close to me and remember to be grateful for the good things in my life.
- I must realize that we should see the positive and the negative side of things all the time.

My development roadblocks:
I sometimes do too much daily and struggle to keep my energy up. I have difficulties expressing myself clearly to people when I feel tired. My progress is slowed by others' lack of participation, lack of energy, and lack of interest in my activities.

People can help me develop around me by:
People can remind me to rest. People can suggest activities or projects that complement my interests or help me connect with people. People can remind me what to focus on when losing sight of my interests and responsibilities toward others.

Myths about the Enthusiast Type

People believe that Enthusiasts always follow their interests. However, the Enthusiast does not always follow his or her source of enthusiasm but follows it when it feels right. Another myth about Enthusiast types is that they have limitless energy; on the contrary, Enthusiasts have limited energy like every other personality type. Many people believe they can't keep commitments, but Sevens can be counted on sticking with a situation or job.

Another myth about Enthusiasts is that they always oppose rules; people with Type 7 personality sometimes has a reluctant attitude toward rules. However, Sevens like rules if they relate to their interests or passions. Some people claim that the Enthusiast types are lazy and aimless. On the contrary, Enthusiasts have strong powers of concentration and can concentrate on a task for hours. Also, Enthusiasts often take the initiative when others need assistance or guidance, but they may be careless when performing a task or job if it's their hobby. Sevens sometimes take many tasks simultaneously but like to focus on one project at a time and do their best to finish them on schedule.

Where Enthusiasts Excel

Enthusiasts are, according to their type name, enthusiastic about many aspects of their lives. They generally enjoy going out and exploring new things and meeting people from different parts of the world. They often have a lot of energy for life and enjoy living in the moment. Enthusiasts are usually responsible, giving them a good edge in the workplace.

Enthusiasts are good at connecting with people and motivating them to participate in similar activities. Because of their versatility and desire to learn, Enthusiasts are exposed to many situations and people. As a result, they have plenty of opportunities to expand their knowledge and social circles. Careers that Enthusiasts work best at are entertainers, politicians, entrepreneurs, marketing and sales, and artists if the job they are enthusiastic about relates to their work.

Type 8: The Protector

The Protector type is confident and in control of their responses, but they can be cold or harsh when confronted with an emotional situation. They have a limited time to reflect on their decisions and tend to be less self-reflective than other Enneagram types. Protectors usually have a lot of internal energy and are motivated toward success, so they quickly make decisions aligned with the person's values. They are generally low in self-esteem, which hinders their confidence and self-assurance.

Type Connections

Wings: Enthusiast, Peacemaker
Security type: Helper
Stress type: Observer
Non-Connection Types: Skeptic, Perfectionist, Lover

Type Description

The basic principle I did not take into account for:
Everyone has a sense of innocence and truth as a core belief in their lives.

Instead, I grew to believe:
Some people take advantage of others. There are negative intentions behind every action or situation.

As an outcome of this belief, I adapt by:
I stand by my truth and hiding my weaknesses so that others will not take me lightly. I guard my space by not letting others get too close. I fight to protect other people against my enemies.

Main Characteristics

As a result of this practice, my focus is on:
I tend to avoid confrontation; instead, I show discontent indirectly and declare my power toward others early on.

I put my energy in:
I have a lot of energy reserves that I can distribute when needed to make sure that others will not get close to me. I often feel guarded against negative people or circumstances. I can stand firm in the face of adversity.

My good qualities:
I tend to protect weaker people, and I fight for a cause I believe in.

How I talk with people:
I am headstrong and unwavering. Sometimes I cut the weak when defending my status quo. I like to confront people directly with my stance, and it is hard for me to convince them of my view. I often dismiss people's ideas or concerns that seem dangerous to me.

My Types' Discomfort

These things bother me:

I become stressed when people take liberties with my values. I get stressed when challenged in my comfort zone. I am easily angered and defensive when people question my decisions or my way of doing things.

These things make me mad or sad:
People that try to interfere in the spotlight that I get because of my position or abilities irritate me because I feel that they get more attention than I do. People that do not seem to respect me annoy me very much. People that take advantage of me bother me because they deceive me or ignore my opinions. People that say one thing and do another bother me because they are deceitful. People that give up easily irritate me because they seem unreliable.

How I express my frustration and dissatisfaction:
I stay calm when pressured because my responses are determined by my internal values, not external circumstances. I dig my heels in and refuse to retreat when I am angered or criticized. I hide my disappointment when things get difficult or when I feel cornered. I only show my anger indirectly so I can control the situation calmly. I lose control in situations that trigger my anger. I maintain excellent composure, and I stay clear-minded when under stress.

Body-Mind-Spirit Journey as a Protector

My spiritual journey is:

My purpose is to follow my values and practice unconditional love. I believe that we are all interconnected, and we must practice unconditional love toward ourselves and others, which merits their respect.

My path as a Protector is:
My path is to continue strengthening my sense of purpose and aligning with my values. My path is also to strengthen my sense of unconditional positive regard and practice becoming more openhearted with myself and others.

My body as a Protector brings me:
Fatigue and migraines tend to build up when tension is high in situations I am in.

Responsibility as a Protector

My internal critic says:
I protect others even though they are not worth protecting, but people are tired of my strictness or my authority. People either depend on me or cringe when I appear.

Personal Development

My goal to develop myself:

It is helpful to have a clear understanding of others' intentions so I can make appropriate decisions. I need to reach for excellence to protect others. I must communicate honestly, with an open mind, and without distorting the truth. I need to remove my critical and defensive approach toward others to help them participate in the process.

How I can develop myself further:
- I must follow my values and help people take charge of a situation to become successful.
- I need to show people that they can become strong in their challenges.
- I need to become decisive and eliminate anything in my life that compromises my effectiveness. I must ensure my balance by continuing to have time for myself, as I need a clear mind to help others.
- I need to accept myself and others as they are. I need to accept my limitations and strengthen my sense of trust. I need to understand myself better and accept my uniqueness; otherwise, I will feel isolated.

My development roadblocks:
I do not like to be controlled. I am not aware of when I control others in their decisions and often deny it from happening.

People can help me develop around me by:

106

Give me feedback when I need it most. Build boundaries and limits on things I can protect them from or not. I also appreciate people that help me open up when I feel vulnerable.

Myths about the ProtectorType

Eights are often perceived as aggressive, tough, and excessive, but they can be quite reserved and quiet. They are often misinterpreted by their loved ones or the people around them. Eights can be too focused on themselves or their interests to pay attention to others' problems. Eights usually do not see problems with their personalities or practices, but they need feedback from their loved ones to realize how their behavior affects people around them.

Where Protectors Excel

Eights are some of the most independent types in the Enneagram system, they like to work independently and often create alone. They value personal achievement and like to be independent. They like to learn and interact with the world through work and school. Eights can manage their time well and have exceptional attention to detail.

Type 9: The Peacemaker

Type 9 personalities view the world through a place of peace and harmony. They like to keep a low profile and do not often raise their voices or display tempers. However, they may become irritated by too quiet and passive people.

Because they seek harmony and balance in life, they often set an example for others to follow. The Peacemaker type wants people around them to be happy and tend to avoid conflicts and arguments. For this reason, they are reliable and trustworthy.

Type Connections

Wings: Protector, Perfectionist
Security type: Achiever
Stress type: Skeptic
Non-Connection Types: Helper, Enthusiast, Lover

Type Description

The basic principle I did not take into account for:
Everyone can get along well by understanding each others' needs.

Instead, I grew to believe:
Society has divided the people and has made it unfair for others to get what they need. In return, we all should be the ones to understand each other's needs, and we should be the ones that look out for each other.

As an outcome of this belief, I adapt by:

I serve as the middleman to others. I often settle in the middle of any situation to ensure I do not build biases or choose sides.

Main Characteristics

As a result of this practice, my focus is on:

I must understand both sides of the story or a situation. I must be careful not to pick sides or create bias. I must listen to the individuals and make sure their concerns are satisfied. I am neutral in effecting change. I am open to hearing all sides of a situation before deciding.

I put my energy in:

I prefer people not to be too demanding, emotional, or outspoken. It is easy to compromise with people when they agree to be reasonable about a situation or solution. When I sense that there is conflict, I let someone go first. I try to reveal only the solution when I must speak on a topic.

My good qualities:

I am fair in all aspects. I maintain an open mind in hearing both sides even though I am prone to be objective in my judgments. I can tolerate being misunderstood and not judged. My people-pleasing tendency helps me keep good relationships with others. I am very agreeable and respect compromise.

How I talk with people:

I am mostly non-confrontational and friendly towards others. I like to listen more than talk. I avoid confrontation and arguing.

I like to solve problems peacefully rather than confront them. I avoid taking sides and judging. I try to find solutions to a problem and avoid conflict. I give in too easily to people and avoid getting upset. I back down, avoiding a topic or speaking for myself, as I do not want to lose someone's attention or trust. I become sensitive when someone criticizes me.

My Types' Discomfort

These things bother me:
I can become withdrawn or preoccupied when criticized. I can be evasive or defensive, and I tend to be critical of myself as well. I can complain or feel sorry for myself when I feel criticized.

These things make me mad or sad:
I tend to take things too personally, and I worry when I am judged unfairly. I blame myself and withdraw when someone is harsh with me.

How I express my frustration and dissatisfaction:
I prefer to avoid becoming angry. I might say or do something in a joking manner instead of becoming sarcastic.

Body-Mind-Spirit Journey as a Peacemaker

My spiritual journey is:

I want to serve and help people live a good life. I value peace and harmony and tend to avoid stressful situations.

My path as a Peacemaker is:
I value balance and harmony in life. I try to avoid arguments and conflicts, and I stay away from stressful people and situations. I try to maintain a balance between all the situations that I encounter.

My body as a Peacemaker brings me:
Illnesses like chest pain and muscle cramps build up when I feel tense. I perform better when I focus on peacefulness and harmony.

Responsibility as a Peacemaker
My internal critic says:
I'm not being fair to others. I'm giving up too much. I'm ineffective in solving conflicts. I must not let go of the side I favor. My inner peace is shaken if I show favoritism and do not listen or understand both sides.

Personal Development

My goal to develop myself:
I must become better at listening and being aware of what I need and when I need it. I must learn to speak up for myself in

a confident manner and avoid withdrawing or feeling defeated whenever I am confronted with conflict or criticism.

How I can develop myself further:
- I want to be balanced, and I want to be fair in every situation.
- I must become better at holding back from defending myself or worrying about what a person thinks of me.
- I want to become a better problem solver and arbiter who helps all those involved meet their needs.
- I need to give more support to form a trusting relationship, especially with people I feel close to.
- I want to be more confident and assertive when I feel persistently pushed around.

My development roadblocks:
I understand communication, but I can be too sensitive and defensive.

People can help me develop around me by:
Encourage me to show my point of view. Allow me to acknowledge my emotions and set boundaries. Getting support is important to me, especially when I make responsible decisions in my life. Let my take on a situation be heard without personal attacks or judgments.

Myths about the Peacemaker Type

Nines are often considered lazy, slow, unproductive, and lacking in leadership and effectiveness. On the other hand, Peacemakers put their energy toward people's feedback. They are often known as effective leaders but are often underestimated because they are quiet. They do not like confrontations and appreciate others' points of view to help them better understand themselves and how they enact their roles. Nines are often accused of burying themselves in their feelings, which is not true. Nines simply allow their feelings time to manifest and understand it when they arise. They are not as quick to judge their feelings and need to process them with others.

Where Peacemakers Excel

Peacemakers are flexible people who can get stressed when confronted with emotional situations or do not know what to do. They are sometimes impatient with people who don't follow their judgments, so they have difficulty connecting with others, including their children. Peacemakers tend to know what they're doing and are prepared to deal with ever-changing situations.

Nines believe they must practice creative calm and balance their energy with others. They are exceptional at bringing people together and motivating them to achieve goals. Peacemakers are diplomatic and can resolve conflicts effectively. They may take time to build trust for people they interact with but are often unaware of it. Nines do not like to lose or be defeated and prefer to achieve victory through positive energy. Regardless of their initial reactions, they always look for a positive outcome.

Chapter 8: Personality Type Differentiators

The Enneagram has 36 type connections, to which two main personality types share a wing or a security-stress connection. Knowing two people with similar or different traits can affect how they approach life is extremely common.

Knowing your personality makes you learn more about yourself and how you can change, grow and improve yourself to become a better person. The enneagram is one test that can help you identify your character traits and give you ways to improve yourself. Personality is a combination of your character and your inner self. It affects your behaviors and responses to stimuli and stress in your environment. Different personality types have different behavioral traits; this is why you experience the way you do in certain situations, places, and with people.

Research has shown that adult personality has its roots in early childhood and could be linked to our genes, environment, and heredity. The enneagram has been around for a long time and is scientifically proven to help change behavior and helps people become happier people because of their effective results. This is to be aware that there is a right and wrong way of using the Enneagram, just like any other test. This book covers things that are important for you to know beforehand to make the most out of your experience with the personality.

115

Communication and personality are two of the most important aspects of having a good relationship with your partner. Knowing each other's personality lets you know what works and doesn't with the other person. Acknowledging your differences is important. If you both know these complimentary traits, it can allow you to grow and improve a relationship.

The Enneagram can help you understand why you react or respond at certain times. If you have high self-confidence, you can take that factor into your decision-making and actions to make more informed, confident choices. Knowing your personality can help you prepare for certain situations and make them less stressful and chaotic for you in advance.

Understanding your strengths and weaknesses is important for your personal development. Knowing your personality can help you understand your tendencies to find ways to work in your favor. You can also find ways to incorporate strategies into your work life and personal relationships, like improving your communication skills, depending on your strengths to find the right career path, and much more.

Your personality can influence your relationships with your parents, children, co-workers, and friends. Your personality can influence. The test asks you to answer some questions, giving you your trait results. You can compare your results with friends and other people you know to see how similar or different you are from them. Knowing these traits can help you create and develop healthy habits.

Perfectionists

- Perfectionists and Helpers are similar because they focus on others' needs and repress their own. They differ because Perfectionists are more self-sufficient, and Helpers are more relationship-oriented.
- Types 1 and 3 are goal seekers, but Perfectionists are more motivated by their inner critic, while Achievers are driven by their inner motivation to succeed. The difference is that Perfectionists are more likely to be harmed by their inner critic, which drives them to do what is right in the eyes of the critic's high standards. At the same time, Achievers are more determined to succeed and to transform their image and attitude, even if it means taking corners to get there and be rewarded for their successes.
- The Perfectionist and the Lover share some personality traits, but the Perfectionist's idealism is more concerned with correct behavior and "getting it right". Meanwhile, the Lover's idealism revolves around possibilities for ultimate fulfillment.
- Types 1 and 6 are look-alikes, but Skeptics doubt and try to gain a sense of safety and certainty, while Perfectionists prevent mistakes and correct what is wrong.
- Perfectionists and Enthusiasts are idealists who want a better world, show intensity and helpfulness, and value self-reliance. However, Perfectionists are serious and self-restrained, while Enthusiasts are fun-loving and expansive.

- Types 1 and 8 are similar, but Protectors express their anger directly and go from impulse to action in a snap. Perfectionists, however, hold their negative emotions until a sense of doing what is right floods them and reveals how they feel.

Helpers

- Types 2 and 3 are similar in that they both focus on helping others; Type 3, the Achiever, focuses on tasks and goals and getting recognition for their accomplishments, while Type 2, the Helper, gets their sense of achievement from the emotions that overwhelm them.
- Helpers and Lovers are Heart Center types, sensitive, relationship-oriented, helpful, emotionally intense, and attuned to feelings. Helpers feeling secure become more internalized, self-oriented, nostalgic, and uniquely creative, while Lovers under stress become more pleasing, outer-directed, focused on others, and giving.
- Types 2 and 5 are look-alike types sensitive to the claims and needs of important others but differ in how they sustain the giving mode. While the Helper moves forward to attend to peoples' needs and often loses their boundaries, the Observer disconnects to recharge their personal space.
- Helpers and Skeptics are similar in that they both focus on the needs of others and feel indispensable. On the other hand, Helpers move forward with vibrant energy,

while Skeptics please other people to gain safety and certainty.

Achievers

- Types 3 and 4, Performers and Lovers, have some personality traits in common but differ in that Achievers sustain a go-ahead goal orientation. In contrast, Lovers have difficulty sustaining a goal orientation.
- Types 3 and 5 are similar in that they are oriented toward tasks, objectivity, competency, activities, and getting things done and detach from their feelings.
- Types 3 and 7 are look-alikes because both are active, assertive, upbeat, task- and activity-oriented, and often overbooked.

Lovers

- Types 4 and 5 are analytical, reflective, sensitive, shy, and appear superior. However, Lovers are on the emotional side, and Observers are a more detached type.
- Types 4 and 6 are similar because they both question situations and magnify them, oppose authority, get reckless, break the rules, defy dangers, and have periods of self-doubt.
- Types 4 and 8 are similar because they show intensity, depth, directness of expression, a desire for authenticity,

and tendencies toward recklessness, impulsivity, and opposition.

Observers

- Observers and Skeptics are similar in that they are analytical, reflective, thoughtful, hesitant to take action, and retracted. However, Observers can detach from circumstances, while Skeptics have difficulty doing so.
- Observers and Enthusiasts are Head Center types that share some personality traits. Observers avoid painful feelings, while Enthusiasts seek positives, express their desires, and spurn boundaries and limits.
- Observers detach from feelings and judge intellectual matters only. Perfectionists are intense, suppress their desires, and seek to improve themselves and others. These traits make Type 1 and Type 5 very similar.

Skeptics

- Types 6 and 7, Skeptics and Enthusiasts, are similar in that they are analytical, imaginative, and able to connect diverse ideas.
- Types 6 and 8 can be considered look-alike types because both can be aggressive, challenging, and confrontational. Differences arise in how the two types

take action, with Skeptics seeking certainty and Protectors always having it.
- Achievers and Skeptics share some personality traits, but Achievers are more questioning, reflective, and trusting in others to get things done. Skeptics need to mobilize for action, while Achievers sustain a goal orientation.

Enthusiasts

- Types 7 and 8 are self-assertive, have little inner restraining force, and are pleasure-oriented. Enthusiasts avoid pain, explain or rationalize difficulties, escape conflicts, and go into future planning.
- Types 7 and 9, Enthusiasts and Peacemakers, can be look-alikes because they want life to be pleasant, upbeat, and avoid conflict.
- Enthusiasts are oriented toward themselves and their likes, wants, and needs, while Helpers are oriented toward others and their emotional needs.

Protectors

- Observers and Protectors are similar in that they value respect and truth, resist control, become possessive of space and key resources, and are curious. However, Observers are more retracted, contained, and measured, while Protectors are more expansive, expressive, and excessive.

- Helpers and Protectors share some traits, but Helpers use their vibrant energy to move toward others with a strong sensitivity to others' feelings and needs. In contrast, Protectors use their big energy to act forcefully.
- Achievers and Protectors are similar in that they are assertive, goal-oriented, and willing to take charge. However, Achievers ' anger comes up more when they feel obstructed.

Peacemakers

- Types 1 and 9, Perfectionists and Peacemakers, have similar personality traits. However, Perfectionists hold to their positions and standards, while Peacemakers readily adapt to others' positions, often losing sight of their own.
- Types 2 and 9 are look-alikes because they both focus on pleasing others and meeting their needs, but Peacemakers are more reactive and blend in to make things comfortable without changing their image.
- Types 3 and 9, Performers and Peacemakers, are similar: both are personable, practical, amiable, competent, and depend on external support and approval. Mediators are slower-paced, readily accommodate the opinions and claims made about them by others, and substitute others' agendas.
- Types 4 and 9, Lovers and Peacemakers, are both relationship-oriented, caring, and empathic, but they

differ in that Peacemakers are oriented toward others and like to blend in.

- Types 5 and 9, Observers and Peacemakers, are considered look-alike types because they can be retracted and introverted, thoughtful, discreet, and may even seem invisible.
- Skeptics and Peacemakers share some personality traits. Still, Skeptics are more at ease, relaxed, and accepting of life, while Peacemakers are fearful, questioning, wary, and mobilized for action.
- Types 8 and 9 are both Earth-Center types and enjoy earthy pleasures. However, Protectors welcome conflict and anger, while Peacemakers avoid conflict and anger.

Chapter 9: Embodying Your Personality Type

Do you shift into the stress type connected with your personality type when you are under stress? Do you shift into the security type connected with your personality when you feel relaxed and secure?

You can use the Enneagram Personality Test to determine your personality type and then ask someone else to verify your choice. Find someone you trust to give you an honest answer and if you know that you are open to other types of opinions. You want to choose someone who is neutral and will not be convinced of your self-image about your own personality. I believe you may want to lie to yourself regarding your personality type. It is challenging for most of us to realize our own personality type because it is part of our own internal identity.

Your personality is a part of your identity. How you act and feel in relationships is influenced by your personality type with your spouse, young children, and friends, as well as work circumstances. Observing your thoughts, feelings, and body experiences help you discover your Enneagram personality type and to facilitate your personal development. Self-observation practices are essential to personal, professional, and spiritual development and personality management.

This chapter provides the following guides and exercises:

- a maximum self-awareness guide for sensory awareness; and
- breathing and centering exercises on developing self-observation.

Remember that sensory awareness and self-observation are psychic training to condition your mind and reach your optimal goal; it is like learning a new language or playing a musical instrument. Suppose you can learn this language or instrument. In that case, you will be able to communicate with and express yourself in life as you develop your ability to observe your behavior, thoughts, and feelings. This is the first step in practicing mindfulness and creating healthy boundaries in relationships.

Maximum Self-Awareness Guide

You can apply this guide to any situation to center yourself and become present at the moment. Here are the steps:

1. Make a mindful intention to observe yourself.
2. Do an internal reality check. Are you breathing deeply? Are you feeling relaxed? Are you sensing any tension in your body? Are you calm or anxious?
3. Observe the physical sensations of your body by closing your eyes and using your senses to observe whatever images come into your awareness.
4. Observe physical sensations as you notice your breathing. Observe everything around you and take in all the colors of the objects around you.

5. Bring yourself to what you are doing before this guide and affirm that you can focus on the task.

Grounding and Centering Exercises

These grounding steps can help you center yourself. These can help you keep yourself calm and centered when upset or stressed. You can do this in any position you prefer, as long as you are in a comfortable and quiet place.

1. Close your eyes and take a deep breath through your nose for about five seconds, then exhale about eight seconds through your mouth and not through your nose. Allow yourself to be open, receptive, compassionate, and curious in the present moment.
2. Repeat this ten to twenty times. As you breathe in, feel the air as it fills your lungs. Imagine that as you breathe out, tension is released from your body.
3. Imagine a white light on the top of your head and all around you. As you do so, imagine yourself being grounded by the earth in each breath.
4. Give yourself a few minutes to bring in the sense of centeredness; then, you can resume what you are doing after as you open your eyes.

The following breathing and centering practice can help you undertake the suggested personal and professional development practices. It takes only a few minutes in your day and can help you develop more flexibility, adaptability, and understanding.

126

Principles Related to the Enneagram

In this section, we discuss five principles related to the Enneagram. Each of these principles has three interrelated components.

Three Laws of Behavior

1. Wherever your attention and energy pattern go, your behavior follows.

   - Ask yourself, "How did I stay aware of my energy and attention?"

2. Changing your behavior requires self-observation of your pattern of attention and energy.

   - Ask yourself, "Did I redirect my energy and attention to myself when I reacted to the situation?"

3. Although self-observation becomes easier as you practice it, it never becomes habitual. Self-observation requires continuing practice.

   - Ask yourself, "How do I manage my emotions and energy better next time?"

The three laws of behavior give you guidelines for changing patterns of how people can improve their reactions to their surroundings and handle emotions better.

Three Centers of Intelligence

Western psychology and education have elevated the mind to prominence over the heart and body as the three centers of intelligence.

In the Enneagram, the core types are Types 3, 6, and 9, and each core type has two adjacent types representing variations on the respective core type. While each core type relies on one of the three intelligence centers, depending on which triad it is in. The heart, head, and body centers represent the main emotions that all beings have, respectively: love, security, and worth. People experience pain, fear, and anger when these are not met. These are:

- **Heart Center - for Helpers, Achievers, and Lovers**

  If you are a Heart Center type, you depend on others' approval and respect to support your self-esteem and desire for love and connection. You absorb other people's negative energy and suppressed thoughts, so you don't become vulnerable. You are sensitive to others' moods and feelings, so be aware of possible triggers that can create unwanted emotional responses within you, as well as negative patterns of behavior. You can become overly concerned with others.

- **Head Center - for Observers, Skeptics, and Enthusiasts**

  For Head Center personality types, you rely on others' recognition and approval to support your sense of security and certainty. The Head Center types believe in the "I think therefore I am" concept, expressing a disconnect from the body and emotions. People who use this center more do not like to feel and express negative emotions. The Head Center type characterizes or dismisses feelings associated with shame and vulnerability. You can become judgmental and rigid in your thinking and behavior.

- **Body Center - for Perfectionists, Protectors, and Peacemakers**

If you belong to the Body Center type, you filter the world around you by relying on your gut instinct or physical sensations. These actions help you make sense of the world around you, and you depend on your own accomplishments to fulfill your need for self-respect and self-esteem. Values and significance are found in what you accomplish in life. You also value wealth over other people's approval. The three personality types that mainly use the Body Center do not like feeling and expressing emotions. Instead, their types characterize or dismiss feelings when they start the experience. In doing so, you become disconnected from your physical sensations, which need to be acknowledged for what they are: perceptions carrying important messages. You can become critical and rigid in your behavior and thoughts.

Three Life Forces

Whether or not we are aware, we function from three life forces within us.

- The active force provides the energy for action and expression.
- The receptive force takes in, processes, and digests all the stimuli your senses receive. It is the basis of empathy and compassion.
- The reconciling force brings your active and receptive forces into proportion and is the master force you need to develop.

I have included a prayer for helping you find calmness as you encounter situations using the concept of these three life forces.

"Highest One, please grant me the courage to change the things I can influence, to know what is right and wrong, and to accept things I cannot change."

Understanding these forces can help you understand how you can interact and gain control of your thoughts and emotions. This step should be a continuous effort to help you bring balance to your life.

Three Levels of Learning and Knowing

We all have three ways of learning and knowing. These ways can be useful in understanding yourself and developing your personality.

1. **Knowing Based on Your Habits:** This level of knowing and learning occurs almost automatically through the five senses and requires little personal awareness. This step would ultimately be based on repetition. Once you try it and succeed, it becomes a habit known as subconscious knowing.
2. **Knowing Based on your Awareness:** This includes questioning and reflecting on your assumptions and replacing your automatic reactions with conscious and deliberate choices. This act can help change how you react to stressful situations and relate to those around you.
3. **Direct Knowledge:** This is a way to pursue the transformational level of knowing and learning, where you experience your life without bias. The more you do new actions, the more your understanding of the activity or your knowledge increases. New results drive you to learn and experience more by handling more, creating more knowledge, and learning opportunities.

The ASAs of Growth Process

The ASAs of Growth is a practical, powerful, and personal development model with three components. These steps take your learning experiences from the memory stage and make them available to you when you need them. Learning something once and storing it in your memory is ineffective in helping you adapt or change anything about yourself or your life. You need to do it repeatedly to imprint or anchor the learning and transform it into something you can use in your daily life. For example, understanding ways to improve relationships or develop healthier habits requires continuous practice. The more you do it, the more the possibility of that insight becoming something you can utilize in your daily experience. Through personal growth consulting, you could develop a vision of what you want your life to be or what you want to achieve.

- **Awareness**

Use the breathing and centering practice described earlier to increase your receptivity and grounded presence. This is fundamental to self-observing your adaptive strategy and working with your stress and anger. Gaining awareness helps you focus on your intention and attention to what is happening. This then enables you to make conscious choices about your behavior.

Observe your defensive or reactive reactions by identifying the attitudes that trigger a fight, flight or freeze response. Then, ask yourself about your long and short-term thoughts and intentions for what happens in specific situations. Think about yourself using a positive strategy and choose to go into a different place in your mind to see the benefits and positive outcomes of the situation.

- **Surrender**

Release into acceptance by staying with the experience of letting go and re-experiencing the fundamental principle you lost sight of. This step will help you acknowledge your limitations and expectations, let go of them, and enter into a stage of greater authenticity and mindfulness.

You can readily give up on what is beyond your control and let the process unfold at its own natural pace. Here is a prayer you can use for self-acceptance:

"Highest Being, please grant me the strength to release my struggles and pains that I carry within me. Help me accept myself and my decisions. Let me be more at peace with my truth, accept others' truths, and appreciate your permissive nature of life."

Open your heart to yourself and others to accept whatever arises at the moment. Awareness includes working with judgments of self and others and the associated feelings and sensations. Surrendering to what is happening is a way for you to feel capable of letting go. When surrender occurs, your feelings and sensations are not bottled up. Thoughts and feelings go when there is acceptance. Observe your experiences as they come up and note what you feel and see on the emotional, physical, and energetic levels.

- **Action**

When you notice your reactions, upsets, and distress, pause to collect your energy and contain it. This step will allow you to choose your words and actions. When you discover new thinking patterns, emotions, or transcendence, click a photo or write down a description so you can incorporate it into your own life.

Acting from your insights and understanding is the comprehension stage where you take action from your learning and bring your solutions into reality. This might require a change in your behavior or a different mindset. For example, you can shift from a defense or reactive state to an acceptance and nonjudgmental state. Learn new ways to manage your behaviors and preferences without shame or guilt. You can do the following:

- Practice your ground sense by being fully present to whatever you may be doing, concentrate on your purpose and priorities, and to be present without distractions.
- Practice mindful breathing when your mind has scattered or got stuck in negative thinking.
- Consciously adjust your attitude and behavior by becoming aware of your triggers and making decisions on effective responses and behavior.

Release the need to control yourself by looking at yourself and others without being judgmental or critical. When you liberate yourself from judgments of yourself and others, you may feel a release of energy and relief that you did not have to deal with rejection or judgment yourself. Remember that natural and spontaneous change occurs on its own. Don't force it so that you don't create resistance.

Be truthful as you work through the exercises derived from the Enneagram profile and type. Follow the processes that work best for you and practice initiating your responses and your actions instead of allowing others to lead and direct you. Get out of your way and redirect your energy to being more proactive.

The Enneagram understandings provide ultimate value in helping you to work with reactivity and theme. After a complete cycle of experiencing, accepting, and taking action, you will likely gain more self-awareness, positive energy, and confidence.

Practicing the 'ASAs' of awareness, surrender, and action can help you develop conscious conduct by letting go and taking compassionate and respectful steps.

Chapter 10: Ways to Reflect According to your Personality Type

Choose one practice to work on before moving on to the others. Keep a journal to record your daily responses to these practices. Notice and record the improvements in clarity, focus, and effectiveness after each practice. As you take notes, review and understand any limiting beliefs or emotional blocks that arise. Journaling these thoughts will help you reflect according to your type.

This book will enable you to apply all the principles to your life and develop a sense of its inner meaning. You can become deeply rooted in the principles and begin to live by them, which will help you form a deep understanding of how your mind operates and how to use this knowledge to create a life of happiness and fulfillment.

For Perfectionists

Consider these questions:

- Should I be judging myself and others? How is this helping me positively?
- Has the voice of judgment been constantly present?
- How has my inner critic made me feel?

- How does my body feel it when I am being a perfectionist?
- Is my inner critic affecting my behavior? In what ways?

This practice can be done as often as you notice your reactivity and helps you make life your mindfulness practice. Choose any of the statements below:

- Today, I will practice accepting mistakes and errors as part of life, and releasing resentments when they arise, hence practicing forgiveness.
- Different points of view merit respect from everyone, including myself.
- My inner critic helps me go through life in a positive way.
- My body is sound and can help me make important life decisions.
- My inner critic is helping me by continuously evaluating, measuring, and generally making me a better human.

The ultimate task for Perfectionists is to reclaim perfection by allowing themselves to accept differences and mistakes and to experience compassion and forgiveness toward themselves and others. Begin by forgiving yourself for any judgments you have of yourself and others. Incorporating all of these practices into your life will help you eliminate negative emotions and beliefs from your mind and change your habits.

It will take time and practice before you can combine all these steps in your everyday life. Start today and identify ways in which you are already practicing acceptance and compassion.

Realize the mistakes and miscalculations you have made along the way. Keep in mind that judging yourself and others will keep you stuck in the past. Instead, accept that mistakes occur and focus on the bigger purpose of your life to leave a worthy legacy.

For Helpers

Ask yourself:

- How much of my attention and energy have I been putting into meeting others' wants, needs, and feelings?
- Have I considered my emotions whenever I am present for someone else?
- How much change have I done to myself to meet others' expectations of me?
- How do I feel when I am not appreciated or recognized?
- How did I do today at giving and receiving equally? Did I get caught up in feeling prideful or indispensable?

Practice with these statements:

- Today, I will practice giving and receiving equally by developing my independence and autonomy and by nurturing my interests.
- If I notice a feeling of selfishness or guilt rising, I will pay attention to my wants and needs.
- I am a kind person who naturally wants to care for others around me. However, I must remember that sacrificing my own needs for others is not helping me become a better person, nor is it helping them to become better people.

- Being present for others often means letting go of my ego and no longer listening to my inner critic.
- Taking care of myself is my main priority. I will put this at the forefront of my practice because I know and support others.

Helpers, by nature, commit their energy to help others in need. They are people-oriented types. Their inner critic is often present to guide their actions and stop them from experiencing feelings that are not compassionate or healthy. This happens because the self-critical voice within Helpers arises from and fuels an addictive process in their minds. A Helper's ultimate goal is to make sure that everyone's needs can be met and that being loved and receiving approval are not dependent on how much you give.

To be healthier, Helpers must remember that there is a reciprocal relationship between self-care and compassion for others. They must also realize that to take care of the people around them, and they must first take care of themselves. Often, Helpers find that when they are the most stressed about others' needs, their own needs are not being met. If the inner critic is present, it will always force them outside the realm of compassion. Practicing healing mantras related to the intention to take care of themselves and others will help them separate compassion from selfishness, honor their needs, and do what is best for all involved. This is the ultimate practice of awareness for Helpers. It also frees them from control by others by saying yes to who they are and spending time with those they love, on their own, and doing unpleasant or selfless tasks.

For Achievers

You can check yourself with these questions:

- How have I been addressing how I feel?
- Have I been acknowledging my emotional state when I accomplish something?
- How much work have I been putting on to make others recognize me?
- Have I considered my health when finishing tasks? If not, how can I fix it?

To check your progress, notice if you are listening to others and are aware of your feelings. Once you know the answers, repeat these statements to yourself:

- Today I will practice letting go of constant doing and becoming more conscious of what I need to do.
- I will take my time in accomplishing tasks and allow them to be completed without rushing through them.
- I will be recognizing my abilities instead of comparing myself to others. I will stop competing with anyone.
- Today I will practice accepting my limitations. I will stop trying to be what I am not.
- Today I will respect the boundaries of others. I will take my time well to get things done and avoid hurting others' feelings.

By adopting these practices, Achievers can start to create an inner environment of balance and harmony. They can create spaces in their lives that work for them with the help of their intuitive gifts. At work, for example, they must learn to delegate, focus on their development, and do work that has a deeper meaning.

Achievers get much of their self-approval from external achievement. However, their self-judgment is subtle and hidden under their achievements. They tend to be hard on themselves and live in perpetual anxiety about their shortcomings. However, they can start to practice saying yes to themselves and surrendering their need always to succeed. People with personality types similar to the Achiever need to understand the principle that everything works naturally according to universal laws and that recognition and love come from who you are, not what you do.

For Lovers

Stop several times a day to reflect and consider what you are missing, then ask these questions:

- What have I been feeling disappointed about?
- How was my attention taken by what is missing and not by what is present?
- Have I abandoned my self-love for the sake of others' happiness?

- How do I respond after I let someone prioritize their emotions over my own, resulting in me being offended and upset?

This practice can be done several times a day to reduce reactivity. It uses the "3As" process. Afterwards, recite the following statements to yourself:

- Today I will practice living in emotional balance by appreciating what is positive and meaningful in the flow of life.
- Today, I appreciated what was present and fulfilling in my life, and experienced more of a sense of wholeness.
- Today I allowed myself to find fulfillment and give attention to my feelings. I acknowledged my feelings when I took the time to examine what was positive about my life.
- Today I will experience distinct moments of gratitude and joy in my life. As a result, I will feel better about my life and be able to handle things with more awareness.

The laws of attraction are simple: whatever you give your attention to grows stronger in your life. If you pay attention to what is negative about this life and what you miss, you will get more of the same. The opposite is also true—if you pay attention to the positivity in your past and your happy memories, it will help you create them in the present. Lovers need to realize that a sense of wholeness and love comes from appreciating what is already present in the here and now.

With discernment, you can realize that your intense emotions come from an inner sense of loss. That loss comes from thinking about what you lost in the past or worrying about your future. By becoming conscious of this process, you can start to open yourself to what is present in this present moment. This practice also helps you learn to let go and strengthen your tolerance for uncomfortable emotions like fear, doubt, and sadness.

In managing their lives and relationships, Lovers focus on people's feelings and needs. Frequently, they neglect their self-care due to being obsessed with the pursuit of feeling safe and loved. However, they can start practicing spending more time on self-love and stepping outside what feels good. If you are someone who focuses on the welfare and happiness of others, ask yourself: "What would it take for me to express my needs?" Focus on and pay attention to those who express care, not those who criticize or reject you.

For Observers

You can ask the following questions to your inner critic:

- How can I keep myself from being detached to emotions?
- What can I do to be more compassionate toward myself and others?
- How can I feel emotions without being overwhelmed?
- How could I express my feelings in a healing way?

Pay attention to how you tend to disconnect from your feelings and others. After this, say the next statements to yourself:

- Today, I will practice being more connected with the world around me.
- I will practice being more attentive to others' feelings and be more in-tuned with their needs.
- I will discover my source as the source of all.

If you find yourself retracting, realize that this robs you of energy. Observers need to reclaim the principle that everyone has an ample supply of knowledge and energy and that staying connected with their feelings does not deplete them. You must learn to access your inner wisdom from your body and know when to stop caring so much about what others think or say about you.

Observers have a problem with feeling connected to their emotions. Often, this manifests through feeling empty and unfocused. Remember that when Observers practice self-forgiveness, they say yes to who they are. This inner work helps them be more compassionate and kind to themselves, their soul family, and others around them. It will also show them the path to healing.

Connecting yourself to your emotions will make you more attuned to your physical energy and the cues it gives you. It will also help you restructure your relationships with other people. You need love to feel fully alive. Find people in your life who can help you find love and compassion in yourself and others.

For Skeptics

Stop imagining worst-case scenarios and consider the following questions several times a day:

- Is there a chance I will succeed and regain a sense of peace and balance in my relationships or career despite my skepticism?
- What strengths and resources in my life have not been acknowledged or recognized?
- How can I be more open to the possibilities in my life?
- How can I focus on the good things that can happen instead of the opposite?
- Today I will practice acting with faith in myself and trust in others by taking action before I have proof.

Skeptics trust themselves and others when they calm doubt or fear, move ahead despite lingering doubt or fear and accept uncertainty as natural. To cultivate this sense of trust, you need to stop overthinking and living in fear. Remember that you do not have to have all the answers to move forward. You should remain authentic to your beliefs and intuitions even when unaware. Your life will be more satisfying if you are open and honest about your limitations.

Skepticism is close-mindedness and distrust in you and others. Remember that skepticism is a state of mind, not a fact. It is a form of fear and can be a cover for running away from your truth. By practicing kindness toward yourself, you can accept where you are while still forging ahead for your greater good.

You can also be kind, generous, and supportive of those around you who are struggling.

In relationships, Skeptics schedule everything in little boxes: work, family, sleep, and even their health. Often they do not pay attention to how they feel or what they need. Stop and think if you are giving yourself enough time for self-care and making time for other people. Then ask yourself: "What do I need to be true to myself? What am I protecting myself against? " Remember to trust your inner wisdom and intuition when you need to change directions or address something in your relationship.

For Enthusiasts

Reflect on these questions as you go about your day:

- How have I deflected the things that frustrate me?
- How have I let my discomfort with uncertainty get in the way of my relationships or career?
- How can I be more comfortable with uncertainty?
- What holds me back from moving forward?
- How can I be more patient with myself and others?

Consider the following statements:

- Today I will practice staying in the present moment, no matter what frustrations and painful feelings life presents me with, and keeping others in mind.
- I will do my best to recognize my tendency to escape what feels limiting or negative and use that as a signal to continue what I have started.

- Today I tried to keep my attention and energy in the present moment and to consider others' well-being.
- I must express my feelings openly and honestly.
- If I seem to obsess over something, it is probably because I need to make a change.
- I should notice when something starts to limit me or seem frustrating.

Enthusiasts experience themselves as more in-tune with their emotions than everyone else, but they are less in touch with their intuition, which acts as a warning signal of danger. In relationships, Enthusiasts want to heal quickly, see themselves as always right and control others' emotions. Often they want to change other people's behavior because they feel frustrated that they can't seem to change themselves. Even when they want something to change, Enthusiasts have difficulty allowing themselves to have wiggle room. They cannot make changes willingly and blame others for their frustrations or problems.

Enthusiasts disconnect from their feelings and intuition for a reason. Remember to practice self-forgiveness for anything you may have said you regret later in life. Remember that you can always change your future by changing your present. You must regain the principle that life is a full spectrum of possibilities and that they must stay present despite uncomfortable emotions or tedious tasks.

Enthusiasts must understand that emotions are part of who we are, and steering away from them does not make life easier. They often come to regret missing this out later on. Learning to express their feelings is a great path for the Enthusiast to have a content life.

For Protectors

Do a sense check on yourself by asking these:

- Have I shown myself as too strong or too loud for others?
- Have I caused others to stay away from me or withdraw into themselves?
- Have I hurt others' feelings?
- Have I made others feel controlled or had them perceive that I am controlling?
- Have I been hypercritical of others?

Then you can recite these:

- Today, I will be more open to others' different positions and energies and more aware of my natural vulnerabilities and tender feelings.
- Today, I will become open to receiving and acknowledging affection from others and, in return, express my affection to them.
- Today I will stand calmly with my feelings and realize that others may have different feelings than I do.

People with Type 8 personalities can realize that your urge to take charge is just an old habit of mind. For Protectors, feeling vulnerable means being open to accepting love from other people by expressing gratitude, kindness, and affection. When you are open, others embrace you as you embrace yourself. You are not alone in this life. Take the time to uncover your weaknesses and be kind to yourself. Also observe the people around you who may be afraid of expressing any emotions or sharing much about themselves.

Protectors can regain their original innocence and come to each situation without prejudging it. This skill takes time to develop, and it is something you can continue to work on for the rest of your life. Protectors may become encouraged and inspire others by treating themselves with compassion, the idea of embracing a powerful self even if they feel they may be less powerful than others.

People with the Protector personality type usually forget the principle that we can all lead our paths, and this is the ultimate goal for the Protector to learn. Ask yourself if you should say something to the other person or take a different action: "Should I stay and talk to them, or should I leave it alone?" "How might I feel if I do this?" Be cautious of justified reactions that make you feel uncomfortable or threatened, even if they are justified.

For Peacemakers

Pay attention to how much you are accommodating and denying claims made upon you. Then, ask yourself the following:

- How much time have I spent in going along other people's agendas?
- How can I regain focus on what matters?
- How have people been competing for my attention?
- How did I become distracted from my priorities?

Reclaim your personality development by reading the following:

- I will start to notice when I am uncomfortable and avoid going along with others' agendas or diverting my attention to small pleasures or secondary tasks.
- I will practice loving myself in ways equal to my love of others, and I will respect my limits and boundaries.
- Today I will be compassionate with myself and open to others' needs.
- I will develop my vision rather than letting others' opinions determine the course of my life.
- I will listen to others who share my best vision and relax when I have less to contribute.
- I will pursue my passions and find my mission before mediating others in their affairs.

Peacemakers should regain the principle that everyone belongs equally in a state of unconditional love and union. They must reclaim their self-love and sense of importance. Peacemakers must drop their hero worship to become stronger people, ready to accept that they are humans and make mistakes. They are prone to self-pity, self-deprecation, and self-doubt when they need support and love from others. You must remember that depression is a by-product of misunderstandings about your place in the world or other people's important roles in your life.

Today, Peacemakers can recommit to working on their intuition, love, compassion, and humility. They can become more aware of their weak and strong points as individuals and leaders. Regain your attraction for peaceful resolutions and accept that all may become undone if people do not know how to disagree. They must remember that keeping a level head is still the best way to resolve conflict, and putting yourself first is key to a happier life.

59 Positive Affirmations for Developing your Personality Type

Positive affirmations express the belief that a certain thing is possible. They can benefit anyone striving for a goal by teaching them to think positively. Some people read positive affirmations every day to achieve specific goals. You can benefit by repeating these simple statements to yourself to help you overcome negativity and succeed at your goals.

Repeating positive affirmations help you reach any goal you strive for by increasing your self-confidence, building a positive attitude, and boosting your determination. This helps you visualize your goal and realize the importance of reaching it. This can be any goal you have on your mind!

Affirmations can help you reach your goals faster as they are positive thinking. They involve repeating a phrase or statement until it becomes "second nature."

Now relax and calm down as you repeat each affirmation five times in a row for 2 minutes each. You will listen to the affirmation, and there will be a pause of 2 minutes after each affirmation to give you enough time to repeat the affirmation and let your brain process it.

59 Affirmations for Developing your Personality Type

1. I am powerful.
2. I can develop myself to become better.
3. I am responsible for myself and others to become more effective.
4. I commit to stop selling myself short.
5. I go after what I want in life.
6. Do things even when I am scared shitless out of my mind.
7. Try things that scare the hell out of me.
8. I dare to fail and keep on trying anyways.
9. I put myself first, before anyone else.
10. I accept that what works for me may not work for others and that their successes do not impact my success.
11. I wake up feeling more abundance in my life.
12. I continue to see opportunities in front of me every day.
13. I am open to trying new things.
14. I am okay with making mistakes and learning from them.
15. I want to experience life in all its abundance.
16. I am willing to be uncomfortable to learn and to grow beyond my limitations.
17. I am always willing to improve.
18. I welcome wonderful things into my life.
19. I see beauty in everything around me.
20. I let go of what no longer serves me well to free myself up for new opportunities and experiences.
21. I remember to receive and give as I give.
22. I allow others to see your greatness so that you will be an inspiration to them.
23. I am open to receiving all the good things and love that come into my life, and I am grateful for it.

24. I practice mindfulness daily so I can be fully present in all I am receiving right now.
25. I aim to enjoy life to the fullest and receive all that is coming to me.
26. I understand that I have everything I need to live a great life.
27. I understand the importance of taking care of myself physically, mentally, and emotionally to be at my best to serve others.
28. I value my time and build relationships that nourish my soul and heart.
29. I love who I am and what I bring to the world.
30. I am the best version of me I can be now.
31. I am worth loving and loving myself.
32. I accept that I am enough just as I am right now.
33. I accept myself and my flaws but do not allow them to define or drag me down.
34. I recognize that I have the ability and confidence to make positive choices for myself.
35. I stick to my guns and make choices that support my life and dreams.
36. I look inward to see the truths in my life.
37. I aim to partner with anyone who is in alignment with my values.
38. I accept that I am not perfect, and my imperfection is what makes me unique and beautiful.
39. I accept that I deserve to be loved regardless of my past or present mistakes.
40. I accept responsibility for my past and all the choices I have made up to this point in my life, and I am committed to learning from them and moving forward in a better way.
41. I am willing to let go of any struggle holding me back from moving forward.
42. I accept my actions and learn from them.

43. I am willing to let go of my worries.
44. I forgive myself for all my faults.
45. I take responsibility for my happiness.
46. I give my power away when I cannot take responsibility for the outcome.
47. I understand that I am in control of my life.
48. I can change reality.
49. I forgive myself for holding on to my past.
50. I am free to make my life's decisions now, no matter what happened in the past.
51. I acknowledge that I am responsible for my thoughts and actions.
52. I create my reality through what I am thinking and doing now.
53. I release the negative energy that no longer serves me.
54. I make space for the positive in my life to come through in greater abundance.
55. I acknowledge my blessings and allow myself to be thankful every day for what I have today.
56. I consciously create the space in my life for things to change for the better.
57. I set myself up for success by choosing to think positively.
58. I let go of any bitterness or resentment that takes any joy from my life.
59. I let go of any failed opportunities to learn from those experiences so that I may find greater success in the future.

Freebies!

I have a **special treat for you**! You can access exclusive bonuses I created specifically for my readers at the following link! The link will redirect you to a webpage containing all my books and bonuses for each book. Just select the book you have purchased and check the bonuses!

>> https://smartpa.ge/MelissaGomes<<

OR scan the QR Code with your phone's camera

Bonus 1: Free Workbook - Value 12.95$

This **workbook** will guide you with **specific questions** and give you all the space you need to write down the answers. Taking time for **self-reflection** is extremely valuable, especially when looking to develop new skills and **learn** new concepts. I highly suggest you *grab this complimentary workbook for yourself*, as it will help you gain clarity on your goals. Some authors like to sell the workbook, but I think giving it away for free is the perfect way to say **"thank you" to my readers**.

Bonus 2: Free Book - Value 12.95$

Grab a **free short book** with **22+ Techniques for Meditation**. The book will introduce you to a range of meditation practices you can use to help you develop your inner awareness, inner calm, and overall sense of well-being. You will also learn how to begin a meditation practice that works for you regardless of your schedule. These meditation techniques work for everyone, regardless of age or fitness level. Check it out at the link below!

Bonus 3: Free audiobook - Value 14.95$

If you love listening to audiobooks on the go or would enjoy a narration as you read along, I have great news for you. You can download the audiobook version of *my books* for **FREE** just by signing up for a FREE 30-day trial! You can find the audio versions of my books (depending on availability) at the following link.

Join my Review Team!

Are you an avid reader looking to have more insights into spirituality? Do you want to get free books in exchange for an honest review? You can do so by joining my Review Team! You will get priority access to my books before they are released. You only need to follow me on Booksprout, and you will get notified every time a new Review Copy is available for my latest release!

For all the Freebies, visit the following link:

>> https://smartpa.ge/MelissaGomes<<

OR scan the QR Code with your phone's camera.

I'm here because of you

When you're supporting an independent author,
you're supporting a dream. Please leave
an honest review by scanning
the QR code below and clicking on the "Leave a Review" Button.

https://smartpa.ge/MelissaGomes

Made in the USA
Las Vegas, NV
19 November 2023

81129087R00089